CW00607354

YOUR HOME
IN PORTUGAL

Second Edition

YOUR HOME
IN PORTUGAL

ROSEMARY DE ROUGEMONT

Second Edition

© Allied Dunbar Financial Services Limited 1989

ISBN 0–85121–564–5

Published by

Longman Law, Tax and Finance
Longman Group UK Limited
21–27 Lamb's Conduit Street, London WC1N 3NJ

Associated Offices

Australia	Longman Professional Publishing (Pty) Limited 130 Phillip Street, Sydney, NSW 2000
Hong Kong	Longman Group (Far East) Limited Cornwall House, 18th Floor, Taikoo Trading Estate, Tong Chong Street, Quarry Bay
Malaysia	Longman Malaysia Sdn Bhd No 3 Jalan Kilang A, Off Jalan Penchala, Petaling Jaya, Selangor, Malysia
Singapore	Longman Singapore Publishers (Pte) Ltd 25 First Lok Yang Road, Singapore 2262
USA	Longman Group (USA) Inc 500 North Dearborn Street, Chicago, Illinois 60610

No responsibility for loss occasioned to any person acting or refraining from action as a result of the material in this publication can be accepted by the author or publishers.

The views and opinions of Allied Dunbar may not necessarily coincide with some of the views and opinions expressed in this book which are solely those of the author and no endorsement of them by Allied Dunbar should be inferred.

A CIP catalogue record for this book is available from the British Library.

Printed in Great Britain by Mackays of Chatham.

Preface

The European Parliament is the world's first directly elected international assembly. A total of 518 MEPs (81 from Britain) represent 320 million people from the European Community's 12 countries. The Ombudsman's Committee, which receives about 500 individual petitions each year, has taken the unusual step of appointing – for only the third time in seven years – an investigator to examine the problems of property frauds within the Community.

The person appointed to carry out this work is Mr Edward McMillan-Scott, Euro MP for York. He has been asked to investigate this kind of activity in the light of his considerable experience in this field and his report and recommendations will be debated by the full Parliament.

Parliamentary Office
European Parliament
Rue Belliard
Brussels 1040
Belgium

It is a pleasure to commend this, the second edition of 'Your Home In Portugal' which follows on from the success enjoyed by its companion book, written by Per Svensson, 'Your Home In Spain'.

Since a constituent wrote to me in 1985 complaining that he had been defrauded by a Belgian developer operating in Spain, I have been pursuing my campaign for a better deal for foreigners buying property overseas. I have called the campaign the 'Golden Fleece' and each day brings more letters from people all over Europe who have had problems with the purchase of their dream home in the sun.

For many of them, the problems could have been avoided if they had taken the basic precautions necessary with any form of property purchase. This book will help because it is based on experience built up over many years by Rosemary de Rougemont who was inspired in her choice of career by a financial disaster that befell her family and one that is an all too familiar feature of my own post bag.

The advice given in this book will help you to make sure that your purchase does not become the nightmare I have so often witnessed.

Edward McMillan-Scott MEP

Rosemary de Rougemont

Rosemary de Rougemont was educated in Faro and at the French Lycée in Lisbon before returning to England to Westonbirt School. She qualified as a solicitor in London in 1981 and the following year obtained a degree at Coimbra University subsequently being admitted to the Portuguese Bar – the first 'common lawyer' to do so.

After practising with a City of London firm of solicitors, she left to form her own London practice and became a partner in Abreu & Marques, a leading Lisbon law firm. She has also established a practice in the Algarve.

She has been Legal Adviser to the Portuguese Consulate General in London and is active in the Portuguese Chamber of Commerce.

Dedication

For my mother, Josephine Mary Smith and all those others who promoted the Algarve a quarter of a century ago and for my husband, Peter, with fondest love.

Foreword

I'm grateful to David Vessey of Allied Dunbar for giving me
the opportunity to write this book and for his invaluable
editorial help. If the first edition was long overdue, this second
edition has been made necessary by the success of the first
and by recent changes in the law – particuarly the Portuguese
Tax Reforms of 1989. Portuguese bureaucracy has become
yet more exacting in past months, with 1992 approaching.

There's still a great deal to learn about buying property in
Portugal and, although the book is by no means
comprehensive, it will give you at least enough information
to enable you to ask the right questions. And, of course, the
right way to ask them. Do remember that a charming smile
or a helpless look often succeeds in gaining the interest of
local officials and the prospective resolution of your problem.
My mother once obtained a licence for permission to have a
performing band at her Country Club in two minutes – simply
by giving the Head of the *Financas* a most charming smile
and asking 'don't you like a little romance in your life?'.

My thanks are due to my brother, David Neville-Smith, to
Paul Nunn, Credit Manager of the London Branch of the
Banco Totta & Acores, to P A R Newton at Manx Trust in
the Isle of Man, to Richard Cox for his permission to use
his maps and to Jacques Mer of the Association of Foreign
Property Owners, who painstakingly read through the first
edition and made useful comments for this one.

Finally, my thanks to my long-suffering secretary, Carolyn
Watson, for many hours over the typewriter.

Contents

1 Introduction

Portugal's history

For many years, the inhabitants of Manchester have taken much comfort in the saying; 'what Manchester thinks today, London thinks tomorrow'. They would probably find considerable sympathy for this belief from the inhabitants of Oporto, one of the principal cities in Portugal and known for some years as 'the Portuguese Manchester'. They also have a saying which goes; 'in Oporto they work for it, in Braga they pray for it, in Coimbra they sing for it and in Lisbon they spend it'. There's no doubt that Oporto has something of an historic pedigree and it can with some justification claim to be the founding city of modern Portugal. Founded by the Greeks, some two thousand years before Christ, Oporto was the *'Portus Cale'* of Roman times. The name *Cale* was the name of the first city on the left bank of the Douro, the river that flows through Oporto, and it is a corruption of this old name which brought about the modern name of Portugal.

After the Romans, the history of Portugal is largely one of invasion and reinvasion. First the Roman empire fell to the tribes from the north. Next the Suebi conquered the western part of the Iberian peninsula before losing it to the Visigoths, another Nordic tribe (who had taken the rather important precaution of accepting Christianity). In the 8th century, the Muslims crossed the Strait of Gibraltar and started their invasion of the peninsula which ended with its almost entire occupation. The re-conquest by the Christian forces started

almost immediately but it wasn't until the middle of the
12th century that the repossession of Portugal was complete.

That repossession was done with English help and it marked
the start of a relationship which has lasted until the present
day. The official alliance with England (the Treaty of
Windsor) was signed in 1386 making Portugal England's
oldest ally in the modern world.

A world power

It was over the next 200 years that Portugal emerged as one
of the major countries of the middle ages and established
itself as the richest mercantile empire of the time. With its
back to Spain (a country with which it has always enjoyed
a certain rivalry), Portugal could only really look in one
direction and so it gave birth to some of the greatest explorers
of the day. Bartholomew Diaz, Vasco da Gama and Ferdinand
Magellan pushed back the boundaries of the known world
and in their wake went explorers and traders who helped to
make Portugal one of the greatest colonial powers ever
known. At its peak, the Portuguese empire included Brazil,
Mozambique and Angola together with parts of India and
the Far East.

By 1580, though, Portugal's golden age had ended and the
throne passed to King Philip of Spain. Portugal then went
into a long period of gentle decline which continued through
a period of unsettled constitutional regimes until the
monarchy finally came to an end in 1910.

Political change

The new republic was unable to achieve any form of political
stability and in 1926 a military dictatorship was set up which
eventually became entrenched with the coming to power of

Salazar in 1932. His death in 1970, followed shortly after by
the bloodless 'revolution of the carnations' in 1974 marked
the end of Portugal as a colonial power and its emergence
as part of the new Europe.

Today, under the Presidency of Mario Soares, Portugal is
taking its place in the European Economic Community.
Political power rests with the Parliament, the *Assembleia
Nacional*, consisting of 250 members elected every fourth
year together with four mandatories from the overseas
provinces. The last election was in 1987 and this saw the
party of Prime Minister Cavaco Silva of the Social Democrats
win a great victory.

Portugal is still a basically agrarian society but one that is
changing very quickly. At one time, agriculture produced
only 10% of the gross national product but entry into the
EEC in 1986 has brought new life into the farms and other
parts of the economy. Many new projects are now being
funded by the EEC and the amount of capital investment
has grown dramatically. In 1987, Portugal had an economic
growth of almost 5% and much of this was due to the
increasingly important role of foreign tourism.

Overall, Portuguese membership of the European Community
is a good thing for the Community and a good thing for
Portugal. The European consumers will have more
Portuguese products in their shops and at more reasonable
prices. Portugal will gain some important markets for her
products even though she may have to open up her frontiers
to more foreign products.

For the foreign property buyer and owner, the integration of
Portugal into Europe will have important repercussions. We
can expect to see more in Portugal of the products and services
that we have grown used to in our own countries. We can
expect that the difficulties for foreigners in taking up residence
in Portugal and starting work there will be reduced. The
legislation of Portugal is being adapted to the legislation of
the Common Market.

The entry of Portugal into the Common Market could well give a greater impetus to further foreign settlement, particularly on the southern coast. It could become more normal than ever before for those from the colder parts of northern Europe to have a home in this sun-drenched and hospitable country.

The growth of the property market

If you are thinking of buying property in Portugal, then you're not alone. Having seen the success of Spain, Portugal is now rapidly becoming one of the leading destinations for people looking for a home in the sun. Spain of course has had dramatic success. In the last 30 years or so, more than one million people have acquired property along the Spanish Mediterranean coast and with an average usage of three persons per property, it means that nearly three million foreigners are living either permanently or part of the year in Spain. The Portuguese have not been slow to see this development and are now setting out to ensure that they get their fair share of this lucrative market.

It is migration that has taken place and is still taking place. The door opener, of course, was mass tourism, making people from northern Europe more aware of the warmer and sunnier parts of the European continent. Now, with higher living standards and longer holidays, it's a new phase in the development of the affluent society. After buying a house with fridge, freezer, dishwasher, stereo, video and a second car, a home in southern Europe is, for many people, the ultimate luxury.

In 1987, the number of people visiting Portugal was just over 13 million, mostly Spaniards crossing the borders for a quick bargain. In second place, and bearing some kind of testimony to the long alliance between the two countries, came the British with over one million tourists. Hard on the heels of tourism come the residents and villa owners and this particular area of enterprise is starting to grow very rapidly indeed. At the same time, the Portuguese themselves are hoping to learn from the Spanish experience and to keep as much of it under control as they possibly can. It's already strongly felt that a lack of adequate planning has led to the over-development of some parts of the southern coast, principally the Algarve. But Portugal knows that in order to compete with Spain, it has to provide the overall tourist infrastructure of roads, railways and hotels that will speed up the development of the other equally attractive parts of Portugal.

The British move in

The Germans must take the credit for starting the trend as they were the first to see the advantages of southern Europe compared with their cold winters and wet summers. For many years, the British found it difficult to buy property abroad due to exchange control but since these restrictions were lifted, British buyers have taken the lead.

To date, no other nation has bought so many properties as the British and they have flocked to join the Germans, people from the Scandinavian countries and the rest of Europe. Now even the Americans and the Japanese are buying thereby adding to the more than 30 different nationalities that you can find on the Portuguese and Spanish coastlines.

The reasons for buying

One thing you should be clear in your mind about is exactly why you are thinking about buying property in Portugal. If it's just for your own enjoyment then fine. If it's as a short-term capital investment, then perhaps you should think again. The days of cheap labour and low costs are long gone and any idea of cashing in on price rises based on that are best forgotten.

Prices **are** increasing in Portugal but do remember that it is very much an active new housing market. Second-hand housing is not quite so easy to sell because most of the British buyers do their browsing at home (eg at an exhibition in Tunbridge Wells), not in Portugal. It's not at all uncommon for people to move house in Britain either as a result of increasing affluence or a new job and, as a result, estate agencies in Britain are both full and busy. The same is not so true of Portugal where the majority of house owners are either retired or using their property for a three week annual holiday. Estate agencies are a common sight in every British town – there aren't as many in Portugal as a whole, although you will find plenty in the popular parts of the Algarve.

So, if capital growth is your main objective there could be better ways of investing your money. As far as buying Portuguese property is concerned, all the profits are being made by the landowner, the builder and the agent. You are in it for the pure enjoyment, the pleasure, and the sun!

What this book is all about

The purpose of this book is to explain the ways in which you can go about buying a home in Portugal and settling there and will also cover some of the problems that you might come up against along the way. It's not that buying property in Portugal is difficult – but it is **different** and there's a tendency for people buying property abroad to pretend that the differences aren't there. It's very easy when you're on holiday in Portugal, surrounded by people from Britain and being looked after by a friendly English speaking hotel staff, to imagine that part of the UK has mysteriously been transported to the Algarve. Buying property in Portugal may appear to be little different from buying property in England when you are having it explained to you in a seminar in Tunbridge Wells.

However, if you are buying a home in Portugal, the reality is:

- You are buying a home in a foreign country.
- The contract may be in a foreign language.
- The legal system is totally different.
- Portugal still has exchange control.
- Portugal has a new tax system.

Provided you follow the rules, you will have no problems. But in order to follow the rules properly, you must be prepared to pay for expert advice and help. Why omit to do things that you wouldn't dream of forgetting to do if you were buying a home in the UK? Here, you expect to pay a solicitor to ensure that all the legalities are tied up – but some people still buy homes in Portugal without a thought for the legal niceties.

So, if you're thinking of buying – do look for some sensible advice. You've taken the first step by buying this book – there are other sources of help available to you which will make sure that buying your home in Portugal will be straightforward and painless. The Institute of Foreign Property Owners was set up to help people from all over Europe with property purchase and this book is structured very largely on the experience they've gained in Spain much of which is directly relevant to people looking for property in Portugal. In 1987, a complementary organisation, the Association of Foreign Property Owners in Portugal, was founded and membership of this organisation can prove to be very useful.

Many people from Britain have gone to Portugal with great hopes and have seen those hopes realised. They have bought their home in Portugal and for them it has become a source of considerable pleasure. For others – happily, only a small proportion – the reality has been quite different and their dream has been wrecked by lack of preparation and by trying to speed the process up by cutting corners.

In some cases, this has been the result of deliberate fraud – and this, it has to be said, is not necessarily as a result of 'over enthusiasm' at the Portuguese end. Regrettably, a small number of Britons have seen overseas property purchase as an excellent way of relieving their fellow countrymen of their wealth. It's very easy to disguise fraud when you are surrounded with papers written in a foreign language – but that can be even more reason for getting expert help.

The future

The Portuguese are very optimistic about the future of their country. In a survey held at the end of 1987, over half were convinced that they were heading for better times and the reason for this optimism about the future seems to be based on their increasing realisation that their country is a marketable commodity. In 1987, the number of tourists increased by 25% – six million holiday makers visited Portugal.

Among the tourists, the foreign property buyers and owners are playing an increasingly important role. They may well come several times to Portugal to look around before they purchase and the total amount of foreign currency being brought into the country in various ways is quite significant. Their contribution to the Portuguese economy and the all-important foreign currency reserves is important to Portugal.

So, by and large, Portugal welcomes the foreign property owner. But it is two-sided and it is important that everybody coming to Portugal respects the Portuguese laws and traditions and doesn't try too hard to impose his own customs and culture on a country where he is the foreigner. There have been some signs of irritation – in 1986 a law was passed saying that all publicity must be in Portuguese, although this didn't rule out a translation into a foreign language. At the end of 1987, part of the Algarve was 'visited'

by firemen using crowbars and white paint who proceeded
to deal with any signs which offended Portuguese sensibilities.
This wasn't well received particularly by one exasperated
British restaurant owner who wanted to know how 'The
Galloping Major' would appear in Portuguese!

All of this probably has something to do with the Portuguese
character. If you ask a Spaniard whether the Portuguese
have an equivalent for *manana*, he'll probably say that they
have but it doesn't convey quite the same sense of urgency!
The word is *paciencia* – patience. It's not that they don't
welcome change – it's that they don't want to rush things.

You don't have to stay in Portugal for a long time before you
meet the concept of *mais ou menos* (which literally means 'more
or less'). You will find that it's the necessary addition to more
or less any kind of commitment. If you try and get a firm and
exact price from the farmer selling you a piece of land or the
builder offering to build your house, the answer will always
be qualified with a *mais ou menos*. A meeting agreed at 4 pm
mais ou menos may mean at any hour in the afternoon.
Starting work on Monday next week can mean starting at any
day in the coming week, and finishing at the end of May
mais ou menos, may very well mean June, July or August.

You can of course, try and nail your local builder down to a
precise time and he may readily agree to the schedules you
propose. But, of course, things don't always work out that
way and you have to put up with days or weeks of delay.
The builder is not determined to deceive you – he's trying to
please you by agreeing to your schedule. His planning and
sense of time and urgency are only different from yours – he
will say *paciencia* and not see the reason for the hurry.

So, it's better to be safe than sorry and don't do things (like
booking that first all important holiday) until you **know** the
house is finished. When you're fretting over the slowness of
the Portuguese bureaucracy, complaining over the long
queues in the bank or the many stamps or forms you need
when you only want to pay a bill, remember . . . *paciencia*.

Learning to assimilate yourself into the Portuguese landscape is part of the pleasure of having property in a foreign country. Becoming part of a British 'ghetto' is no real substitute for seeing the country in which you've purchased a home or where you've retired and this will only help to ensure that Portuguese citizens and their welcomed visitors can live together for their mutual benefit.

2 Where to buy

The climate

The climate is the single most important reason for people from northern Europe buying property in Portugal. However, Portugal does not have only one kind of weather, it has several different types according to the season and the part of the country.

Generally speaking, Portugal has mild humid winters and hot dry summers. The climate is influenced both by the Atlantic seaboard, the nearby Mediterranean and the Spanish tableland (the *Meseta*). The variations are most dramatic in the rainfall; some of the mountains in the north west of the country receive nearly 100 inches of rain a year while the north east Tras-os-Montes receives only about 20 inches a year. All of Portugal south of the River Tagus has less than 30 inches a year and in the eastern Algarve it is under 20 inches a year.

The northern coast of Portugal (north of Oporto) has some five to seven days of rain per month including the summer. The almost constant wind from the west, cooled by the ocean, keeps water temperatures on the beaches fairly low. Further south, the rainfall is less but it's a coastline which gets rather more fog than normal.

Inland in the north, around the town of Braganca, it's a more continental climate with hot days, cool nights and much less rainfall. This is one of the more mountainous areas of Portugal and a few people even find ski-ing on the higher slopes.

The middle coastal area, around the city of Lisbon, sees higher temperatures than in the north and much drier summers. In July and August, you can expect rain on only a couple of days every month and the sea temperature is that much higher as well.

Finally, further south and round on the Algarve, the rainfall starts to diminish significantly and the temperature rises. The Algarve has the mildest winters with the temperature rarely going below 50 degrees fahrenheit. During the summer, the temperature during the day rises to the low 80s during the day and just dips below the middle 60s at night. And as for rainfall, well that's almost non-existent.

The islands

The islands of Madeira and the Azores also form part of the administrative area of Portugal. Both groups of islands are volcanic in origin. The Madeiras lie about 500 miles southwest of Lisbon off the coast of north Africa. They have a sub-tropical climate which makes them popular with tourists all year round. Madeira, the largest island, and Porto Santo are the only inhabited islands.

The Azores are set in the Atlantic some 760 miles due west of Lisbon and are scattered around an area of about 900 square miles. Their position tends to give them somewhat wet winters with high winds, rather short springs and autumns and very hot, humid summers.

Madeira does not yet feature prominently on the property buyer's list of places to visit. It is an island that is relatively untouched by tourism largely due to the fact that it has virtually no beaches at all (although the island of Porto Santo does have a magnificent beach). This in itself has meant that tourism has been limited mainly to older people and there's a well developed hotel industry. There is a slowly emerging timesharing industry growing up but this has largely been designed to give the hotels guaranteed occupancy.

Where to buy?

Most northern Europeans tend to be familiar with the Algarve which for them means Portugal. But of course, there's a lot more to Portugal than that, with over 500 miles of coastline and literally hundreds of places for the would-be property buyer to look. It's also useful to get your sense of geography straight – if you look at the map you'll see that Oporto (which is in northern Portugal) lies on exactly the same degrees of latitude as Sardinia, Naples, Istanbul and Barcelona – the Costa Brava in Spain is actually north of northern Portugal.

The Costa Verde

In the far north of Portugal is the **Costa Verde**, the 'green coast'. This stretches from the Spanish border to Espinho, just south of Oporto. This is a beautiful stretch of coastline with green pine forests sloping gently down to miles and miles of sandy beaches. Here you will find the towns of Vila Praia de Ancora, Viana do Castelo, Esposende, Ofir and Apulia. Closer to Oporto but still on its northern side, are Vila do Conde, Povoa do Varzim and Arvore, all of them with excellent beaches.

The town of Oporto itself is famous not only as the second biggest town in Portugal but also as the centre of the port wine industry, largely developed by the British and today its biggest customer.

South from the town are Miramar, Praia de Aguda and Espinho, all with beautiful beaches close at hand.

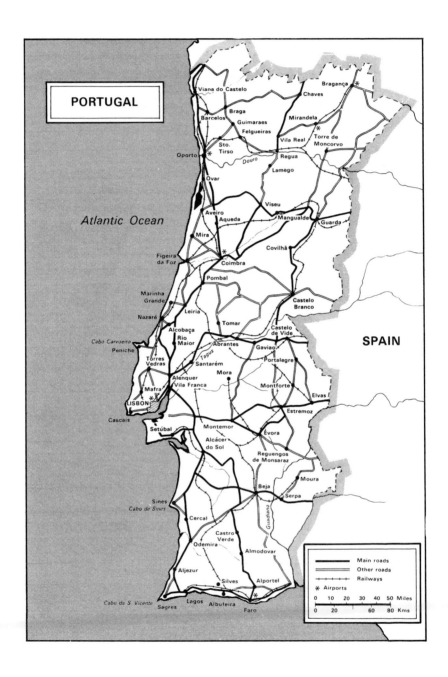

The Costa da Prata

The **Costa da Prata**, the silver coast, starts with the estuary created by the River Vouga just north of the town of Aveiro, crisscrossed by channels and inlets and with miles and miles of excellent beaches. The towns of Torreira and Sao Jacinto are well worth a look and further south you will find Praia de Barra, Costa Nova Praia de Mira and Praia de Quiaios before coming to the town of Figueira de Foz, also called 'the queen of beaches'.

Overall, the silver coast is an area largely undiscovered by foreign tourists with many almost deserted sandy beaches running for many miles along the coastline. There's property within the region to suit most people's requirements but expansion is controlled to ensure that the area doesn't lose its identity. In the coastal area you will find a number of low rise apartments and villa developments capitalising on the excellent beaches.

Further south on the coast are Praia de Vieira, Sao Pedro de Moel and Nazare, the famous fishing village where it's still possible to see the old values retained in the face of the onslaught of tourism. Close by is the cliff-top village of Sitio where there are new properties in or around the town itself and a number of apartments and further developments well suited to family holidays. An area which has recently become extremely popular is that surrounding the Obidos Lagoon. During 1987 and 1988 some major international developers acquired land and are developing this into upmarket resorts.

Even further south are Sao Martinho de Porto and Peniche, Portugal's second largest commercial fishing port. Property here tends to take the form of traditional houses although there are a number of new further developments above the harbour. Close to Peniche are Consolacao and the coastal resort of Praia de Areia Branca where apartments are available.

The Costa do Sol

The third coast is the **Costa do Sol**, the 'sun coast' known locally as the Linha de Estoril. This comprises the south facing coast immediately west of Lisbon with its two famous resorts, Cascais and Estoril, popular as retirement areas for many of the royal families of Europe.

A stretch of coast extremely popular with foreigners, the area has a wide and extensive choice of property. At Quinta de Marinha there's a range of property to be found in this popular area situated on the Atlantic shoreline. Close by are Birre and Malveira da Serra both increasingly popular as residential areas with a range of properties to suit most pockets.

The Costa de Lisboa

The **Costa de Lisboa**, the 'Lisbon coast' (sometimes also called the Costa Azul, the 'blue coast') is the coastline south of Lisbon. Popular places are the Costa de Caparica (which is very popular with tourists), the beautiful town of Sesimbra and the postively idyllic Portinho de Arrabida which is situated at the foot of high mountains with spectacular views across the estuary to the flat finger of sand pointing directly at the town of Setubal. On this sandbank has been built the tourist complex called Troia.

The Costa Dorada

The **Costa Dorada**, the 'golden coast', lies between the Lisbon coast and the Algarve. There's not a great deal of development on this particular coastline but a visit could well be paid to Porto Covo and Vila Nova de Milfontes.

The Algarve

And finally, there's the Algarve itself. Felt by many to be getting over developed, there are still places on this particular coastline that are not that well known. The Algarve stretches from just north of the town of Aljesur, round Cape Saint Vincent and then all the way east to the Spanish border.

The **western Algarve** is generally regarded as the stretch of coast from just west of Albufeira to Cape Saint Vincent. There's not a great deal of property on the Cape but moving towards Lagos is Praia de Salema where a number of new developments are planned including village developments and plots for individual villas. Further along is the town of Burgau which is an attractive little fishing village but one which is becoming more popular having been recently 'discovered'. Lagos itself, centred around the harbour that was frequently used by Nelson, is a popular holiday resort with a range of properties available.

Travelling east from Lagos is Praia de Rocha, one of the first villages on the Algarve to attract tourists. There is not very much property for sale in the centre of the village but there are smaller houses and apartments for sale on the outskirts.

Further east can be found the town of Carvoeiro, which is a busy provincial town. The beach is sheltered with many secluded coves and above the town there are a number of new developments ranging from apartments to individual villas. Close by Carvoeiro is the town of Armacao de Pera with its huge beach, and finally the tourist centre of Albufeira itself with several good beaches and many villas and apartments available for sale.

To the west of Albufeira are Sao Rafael, Coelho, Ponta de Castelo and Praia de Gale all with lovely beaches and in prime development areas. There's a considerable amount of investment going on in these areas and you'll be able to find plots of land for sale as well as villas and apartments.

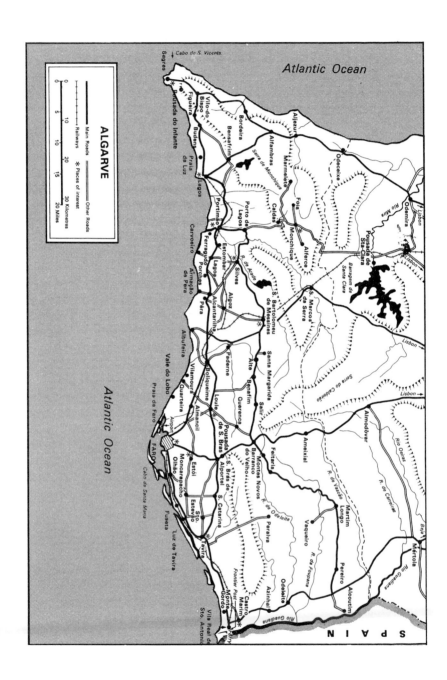

To the east of Albufeira lies the **central Algarve** with its
regional capital, Faro. For many visitors to the Algarve, this
is their main arrival point with its international airport
situated approximately one mile outside the town.

East of Albufeira and on the coastline up to the village of
Vilamoura lie a number of small towns and villages with a
range of property available. The towns of Albufeira and such
resorts as Montechoro, Praia da Oura, Balaia, Olhos de
Agua, Acoteias and Alfamar all provide good facilities for the
visitor and resident with a range of properties available. The
local market town is Loule, but the business centre of the
Algarve is Almancil.

Vilamoura itself is one of Europe's largest residential and
tourist developments. This really is for those people who want
a well organised lifestyle because a huge enterprise is being
planned which will eventually house well over 50,000 people.
Golf courses, marinas and all manner of sporting facilities are
available and this is an area for buying detached villas,
apartment blocks and the occasional individual plot of land.

Next come the heavily promoted (and rather expensive) areas
of Quinta de Lago and Vale de Lobo which are considered to
be amongst the most expensive areas in Europe. There's not
much point in going to Quinta de Lago (except to gaze)
unless you have a rather large chequebook! It's principally an
area of well designed, well appointed, and very expensive
property ranging from small apartments to villas set in their
own grounds. You can expect to find the full range of
facilities including tennis and golf plus every imaginable kind
of water sport.

If it is not essential for you to have your own villa, you will
find a range of good quality apartments and timeshare property
available from some well established British companies.

The **eastern Algarve**, stretching from Faro to the Spanish
border, is comparatively unknown. Many of the towns and
villages have been able to keep their original lifestyle but

property is available and in most cases construction is being tightly controlled so as not to spoil the general atmosphere of the area. There are plenty of beaches but it's an area which is not quite as well served for 'tourist facilities' as the other parts of the Algarve.

The town of Tavira and the close-by fishing village of Cabanas are particularly attractive. Tavira itself was the old capital of the Algarve and is believed by many people to be the most picturesque town in the area. There are some excellent beaches close by and the low hills to the north provide some of the most picturesque countryside in the area. It's possible to find older farmhouse type properties in this part of Portugal and closer to the coast there are a number of individual villa sites as well.

There's also development in the area between Tavira and Cabanas. There are individual villa developments and also some low rise apartment buildings as well.

Further east are the coastal villages of Cacela Velha and Montegordo. Here the lifestyle is very quiet with a small number of villa properties available and land for sale in the area to the north. Finally, comes the last town in Portugal on the Spanish border, Vila Real de Santo Antonio. It has a duty-free shopping area which attracts visitors from Spain as well as those from the eastern Algarve. There will soon be a bridge across the river Guadiana which will give easy access to Spain and will mean that Seville will be less than two hours away by car.

Looking inland

A final thought, of course, is to keep well away from the coastal areas and to look for property in the inland regions of Portugal. If you're really adventurous, you could think of buying an old farm near Braganca up in the Tras-os-Montes in the north-east corner of Portugal. You'll probably have to like growing plants and looking after the odd animal or two but there are still some bargains to be found up in the valleys. Close to Coimbra, you might be able to find an older property in the village of Montemora Velho on the River Mondego, only a few miles away from the beaches.

Or you could go to Tomar, north of Santarem, a town that Somerset Maugham praised as the most beautiful town in the world. And then there's Evora, right in the middle of the plain of Alentejo, and one of the oldest cities on the Iberian peninsula – once a Roman stronghold. East of Santarem, you'll find a range of lakes where property is available and if you're not too put out by the thought of rain and wind in the winter, there's the thought of a home on the west coast near Aljezur on the western coast of the Algarve or even further inland at the village of Monchique up in the mountains with views to the beaches across forests and fertile valleys.

Portugal is filled with beautiful and interesting places so when deciding where in Portugal you would like to buy some property, you've got to start looking at yourself, your character and your preferences. Are you the type for the simple village life or would you prefer the big city? Do you want to live in Portuguese surroundings or in an international community where you can speak your own language?

The choice is yours – and you'll find that Portugal has the choice.

How to get there

Travel to Portugal is not quite so straightforward although the Algarve region is well served by Faro Airport. The other major airports are at Lisbon and Oporto and there are direct flights from London to all three. Naturally, the charter flights tend to go to Faro in the tourist season and it's there that the flight bargains can be obtained.

Travelling by car to Portugal is not one of life's great journeys. The motorways in Spain don't point towards the Portuguese borders and the existing stretches of motorway in Portugal are rather few and far between.

A European motorway is now planned for 1992, linking Portugal with the motorways on the rest of the Continent.

Present day roads in Portugal are acceptable – but time consuming. If you plan to travel to Portugal during the tourist season, you have to be prepared to spend a fair amount of time behind the wheel.

3 What to do and what not to do

The British, having discovered the benefits of Spain, are now turning their attention more and more to Portugal. We now lead the way in foreign tourism with the Algarve being our favourite destination on that part of the Iberian Peninsula.

It was inevitable that the property owner should follow this because Portugal is such an attractive country. The Portuguese are now rapidly waking up to the fact that they have a marketable commodity in the natural attraction of their beaches and coastal regions.

They're also waking up – and so are others – to the fact that selling property is extremely easy. While they may not yet have the Portuguese equivalent to 'the British leave their brains behind at Alicante airport', they are more than aware that a few of us do the most odd things when looking for property in a warm climate.

This chapter, then, is a quick, easy-to-read guide to some of the things you should think about when you're buying property in Portugal. There is nothing particularly magical about any of it. Buying property anywhere can be a hassle at the best of times (it's reckoned to be one of the most stressful activities you can take part in) but, for some reason, we seem to expect it to be trouble free in Portugal just because the sun shines.

Remember, if you were buying property in the UK, you would **probably** go about it as follows:

* You wouldn't necessarily buy the first house you saw and

you certainly wouldn't sign any kind of agreement there and then.

- You would work out what you could afford and you would be careful not to over commit yourself.
- You would want to make absolutely certain that your solicitor had done his job properly and that there were no legal or planning permission problems undiscovered.
- You would get the financial position sorted out **before** you signed the contract and committed yourself to the purchase.
- If the house you were buying was a second home, you would make yourself familiar with the tax position on owning property in addition to your 'main residence'.
- When you were sure that the house was what you wanted, within your reach, legally problem free and that you had the money to buy the house with, then you would go ahead.

Buying property in Portugal is no different.

By and large, people intending to move to Portugal on a permanent basis tend to be a lot more careful about what they buy. It's the holidaymakers and the tourists who, having had a pleasant two weeks in Portugal for a number of years, decide that it might be a good idea to have a permanent base there. Short of time, they take up a few precious days of their annual holiday in order to try and find the house they want. They rush into a decision and then, sitting at home many hundreds of miles away, they simply hope that all the technical problems will be taken care of.

The majority of builders in the UK are decent, honest businessmen. But would you really trust a builder, or a developer, or an estate agent, to undertake all the necessary legal work on your behalf. Most people wouldn't – until they come to Portugal and then for some reason, they think that the rules are different.

This chapter is written for you.

Spending a week at
Hollies holiday home,
x overleat. Jarvis:
having a fab time &
doing everything to
excess!! especially eating
weather glorious have
had an ad twice
in the speed boat
and have attempted
to water ski now
practice needed.

Love
Margaret

Mrs McCourt
20 the Crescent
Solihull
West Midlands
B9.

Be proud
address

20P

LLANBEDROG

Watch your budget

- Don't over commit yourself. If you feel £50,000 is the most you can afford, go for a property costing £47,000 as a cushion against worsening exchange rates. Don't bank on exchange rates getting better – just regard it as a bonus if they do.
- Knock at least 20% off your limit and put that on one side for legal costs, taxes and other costs. It's better to know that your purchase is all above board rather than to have a better range of fitted units in the kitchen. Also, you may have taxes and fees to pay when you buy your property and these can be a significant item.
- Budget your running costs and then only buy property that you can easily afford to maintain (and don't forget you have annual rates to pay as well). Remember, you get paid in the UK in sterling and you have to cope with UK inflation. On top of that, you now have to face a fluctuating exchange rate and Portuguese inflation as well.

Look before you buy

- There is a temptation to make up your mind on the first visit. But it isn't that difficult to make a return trip under your own steam and that would give you a chance to really look at things properly.
- Don't make up your mind in Portugal – make your decisions back home. It's a **major** decision – don't rush it.
- When you go on your first visit, take a camera and plenty of film. You may not get another chance to remind yourself of everything you've seen – photographs will help.
- If you are looking for timeshare, make sure you are

dealing with a reputable company – a member of the
Timeshare Development Association would be a good
starting point.

- Don't be hassled into buying. It's a buyer's market and
  the agents and developers need you more than you need
  them.
- Don't sign anything when you first meet the builder or
  developer. If you like the look of a particular property,
  make sure you return to the UK with:

  — a plan of the property;
  — a plan of the area showing where the property is to be
    built;
  — a full specification (ie the materials with which the
    property is to be built);
  — a full list of the fixtures and fittings;
  — a copy of the contract, in English;
  — a search of the land registry entries (or, failing that, a
    detailed description to enable your lawyers to do a
    search).

- If you feel under pressure to sign some kind of 'intention
  to buy' make sure that you only sign a reservation. And
  never pay over any money.

The legal side

- Do engage the services of Portuguese lawyers and make
  sure you instruct them carefully. They will do as you
  wish but do ask for evidence that it has been done. Don't
  assume that it's all been done for you – get it in writing.
- Don't sign **anything** unless you have discussed it with
  your lawyer first.
- Never pay over any money unless your lawyer tells you it
  is in order.
- Don't sign a purchase contract until you have had it
  checked with your lawyer.

- Open your Portuguese bank account early (you can do it from the UK) and make sure that payments for your property are backed up by an import licence. This will be done by your bank if you ask them and (when your house is finished) they will also ensure that all your regular bills are paid by standing order so that you can then forget them.

Dealing with the vendor

Don't sign a purchase contract that doesn't cover the special needs of Portugal – the following points are to guide you towards some specific problem areas that your lawyer can check:

- It should **explicitly** state that there are no outstanding debts or liabilities on the property or land and that it is not subject to any rental agreement.
- It should not oblige you to pay in a way that gets round Portugal's foreign currency or tax regulations.
- The contract should specify that the building project or urbanisation has been approved by the local authorities.
- If you are paying for your home by instalments, make sure you pay only when the builder completes each stage (and wherever possible reserve the right for an independent check to confirm that each stage has been completed). **Never** sign anything which commits you to payments on a fixed schedule. Your builder may be late – why should you be early?
- It should not require you to pay money to the agent or to anybody other than the person from whom you are going to buy the property.
- It should guarantee that you will get the title deeds and all other necessary documents **at the same time** as you make the final payment towards the purchase.
- It should confirm which services are to be connected to

your property on completion (eg water, electricity, roads).

The list seems rather daunting – but there is nothing particularly unusual to anybody familiar with buying a house in the UK. As we said at the beginning, buying property in Portugal is not different – it's just that people think it's different.

A last word on tax. Make sure you pay all your taxes when you buy your property and make sure you pay all your annual taxes on time. If you ignore this, you are building up problems for the future and it's very simple to appoint somebody to do it on your behalf. Chapter 13 explains the taxes you have to pay on your property – if you don't pay then the authorities are entitled, if all else fails, to sell your property to recover the debt.

You may meet people who tell you that Portugal is a tax haven because nobody bothers to check up on you. Putting a false value in the deeds of your house is 'the Portuguese way of doing things' they will tell you. You are strongly advised to ignore all this kind of 'expert' advice. It may have been true in the past – it is most certainly not true today. The Portuguese tax authorities are rapidly catching up on all kinds of tax evasion and you may find that bending the rules today will earn you a hefty tax bill tomorrow. Under-declaration could result not only in a fine equal to double the tax but also prosecution for breaching Portugal's exchange control regulations.

Stick to the rules – and sleep soundly at nights!

4 The buying process – an introduction

Wherever you are buying property, there are a series of steps that you will have to go through before you can finally move in and make yourself at home:

- In the first place, you have to find the property you want to buy.
- You will have the legal details of conveyancing to sort out.
- Unless it is a second-hand property, you may have some steps to go through in connection with a new property:

  — You may have to buy the land and get the neccessary planning permission.
  — You may need a building agreement with your builder.
  — If you are building from scratch, you will need an architect.

- You will have to pay for your property.
- You will have some taxes to pay.

All these aspects are covered in more detail in chapters 5–8 and 13. They have been written so as to be relatively self-contained but there is inevitably a certain degree of overlap from one chapter to another. In broad detail, what they contain is laid out below – it is suggested that you read these descriptions first as they will guide you to the points you need to bear in mind. The only chapters that are essential reading are chapters 7 and 13 – the chapters on the legal and taxation aspects.

What to buy and how to buy it

Chapter 5 gives you a little more detail on how you can go about finding your property – and some points to bear in mind before you take the plunge.

Dealing with estate agents, for example, is not always as straightforward as dealing with their counterparts in the UK.

The chapter ends with a section on buying your property through a company. This is becoming increasingly popular – though there are some guidelines to follow.

Buying land and building new property

Chapter 6 covers the sorts of things you will need to be aware of if you are buying a plot of land and building your house from scratch (although there are also some useful pointers for any property buyer).

Buying the land

If you are going to build a house, then you have to own the land on which the house is to be built. Once again, there are checks to make (eg never assume that just because it is for sale it automatically has planning permission). It is also a useful section to read if you are buying a house in the course of construction – buying the land first can give you some protection in case your builder hits financial problems.

Planning permission

There are some quite detailed rules on building property in Portugal which have to be followed. If you are building your own home, then your lawyer will have to check all these points for you but even if you are buying a home in a development or in the course of construction, you can't avoid it. You need to know that the builder has all the necessary permits before you enter into any kind of contractual arrangement with him – and this is something your lawyer will do for you.

Dealing with the builder

If you are having a house built there are a number of things to bear in mind when negotiating terms with the builder. The chapter contains a list of useful suggestions but this will be equally useful if you are talking to a developer offering you a partially built property.

Dealing with the architect

If you are having a house designed you will need to talk to an architect about the kind of house you really want to build. We have included a list of points you could ask your architect to bear in mind – but, once again, you will find the list useful regardless of the type of property you are looking for, including second-hand property.

The building contract

This is the formal agreement between yourself and the builder and it will describe the house that the builder is going to build for you. You may find your builder insists on a standard form of contract – it is important to make sure that it doesn't take away your rights under Portuguese law.

Understanding the legalities

Chapter 7 describes the two key stages in the purchase of property in Portugal:

1 The contract of purchase and sale.
2 The title deeds.

This chapter deals with the process that you have to go through to ensure that the agreement between buyer and seller is legally binding and that, at the end of the day, you have good legal title to the property you have bought.

Regardless of what kind of property you are buying, this chapter is essential reading. It also covers the special position on buying apartments and the things to bear in mind if you are clubbing together to buy a property jointly (this is not the same as timesharing which is dealt with in detail in chapter 10).

You and the banks

Chapter 8 describes the financial background to buying your home in Portugal. You will find that it is a very different procedure from buying property in the UK. Portugal still has tight exchange control regulations which only bite when you try to take money **out** of Portugal. It's therefore important that you follow the rules when bringing money **into** Portugal so that you have no problems later on. All property purchase is handled through the Bank of Portugal and they have strict guidelines on the importing and exporting of currency (and this includes special rules on how you may pay a deposit on a property).

The chapter also contains information on setting up and

running a day-to-day current account as well as information on raising a mortgage.

The tax system

Chapter 13 describes the tax system that will affect you as a property buyer. Some years ago, the taxation of property purchase in Portugal (and in Spain, too, for that matter) was a very light hearted affair. The usual procedure was to pretend that your property really cost about a fifth of its true value so as to pay less tax. Some people still believe this happens today.

The best advice is to forget everything you have heard and read chapter 13 carefully. Times have changed.

There are also certain taxes you will have to pay if you live and work in Portugal (or receive any kind of income there) and everybody with property in Portugal is affected by inheritance tax.

Overall, the process of buying property in Portugal looks very complicated. However, just consider how much time you might spend explaining to somebody from Portugal the process that he would have to go through if buying a house in the UK. The reality is that the transfer of property anywhere is always a tortuous process and the best solution is to have a good understanding of what's required and then to get professional help right from the start.

5 What to buy and how to buy it

Introduction

By and large, there are two main ways of buying property in Portugal:

1 You can do it the easy way and buy an existing house or apartment (either a second-hand house or a new one) or buy one that is going to be built in an existing development.
2 If you are much more adventurous, you can buy a plot of land and get a builder to construct one for you.

In this chapter we will be looking at how you can go about searching for property with some thoughts on second-hand houses and new property either completed or in course of construction. If you decide you would prefer to buy a plot of land and build a new house, you will find full details in chapter 6 on the planning considerations together with things to bear in mind in your discussions with your builder and architect.

Many people's 'ideal' approach to housebuilding is always to buy that little plot of land at that perfect spot and build their architect designed house on it. For most people, however, their first approach will be to a developer and to buy a villa on an individual plot or to buy a villa or apartment as part of an urbanisation.

What you decide to buy will obviously depend very much on how you intend using the property. Will you be using it only for holidays or for more permanent residence? Are you buying simply for investment (in which case, as we explained in chapter 1, you might be well advised to think again)? It will depend on the size of your family, your sporting and cultural interests, whether you like sailing and other sea based activities and, inevitably, the amount of money you can afford to spend. Apartments, terraced houses, semi-detached houses with a small plot, village properties with larger plots and building land are all readily available.

Think about selling

The other point you must bear in mind, before you buy, is what you will do when you want to sell your property. Whatever the reasons may be, it will then be very important that the property fits not only your individual tastes and needs but that it has general appeal as well. There has been a 'buyer's market' for the last few years, with many more resale properties on offer than there have been buyers. At the same time, the number of new properties on the market is growing all the time and so it may not necessarily be very straightforward to resell your property in the future. Some types of property, of course, and also some areas, are in such high demand that you get local 'seller's markets' and you will have no difficulty in selling your property at any time. Nevertheless, it is an important consideration and so you should be looking for your new property from a number of different points of view.

If you intend to stay in Portugal for any length of time, it might pay you to buy a small property to start with (and one that can be easily resold), until you are quite sure that Portugal is the place for you. This will also give you the chance to become acquainted with a particular area and will give you the opportunity, of course, to find your final 'dream house'. Some people are even more cautious and start by renting a property for a period, using it as a base for further

investigations before committing any capital. This can often
be a sensible approach – and inexpensive if you rent outside
the main holiday seasons.

How to find the property

There are two basic ways to start looking for a property in
Portugal. On the one hand, you can look at the
advertisements that you will find in many national newspapers
in the UK. On the other hand, you can go to Portugal and
find a suitable property or sales organisation yourself.

The simplest way, of course, is to start by reading the
advertisements in your national newspapers and send for
information on those which appear to be the most interesting.
As you gradually find out more about the various companies
operating in the field, you will find the ones which seem well
established but do make sure to pick up information from
more than one company so that you can compare prices and
offers.

From time to time, you will find that a number of property
companies and other organisations arrange seminars and
exhibitions, often in local hotels. The Algarve Magazine
Exhibition, for example, is particularly comprehensive and
runs not only in London but also in Manchester and other
main centres. If you can get along to see one of these, it
would be a very good opportunity to see first-hand the sort
of properties being offered. Once again, by comparing two
or three such exhibitions, you will gradually get an idea of
those people who really do know what they're talking about
and who have good opportunities to offer you.

Some of it may often have an attractive price if it turns out
that the owner is forced to sell it for some reason or that he
himself bought it some time ago for a good price. But do bear
in mind that older properties may be built with lower quality

materials and they may lack the stricter degree of control in construction that exists today. Repairing an old house with a problem can be expensive.

Alternatively, try and get hold of copies of the local expatriate newspapers from Portugal, most of which carry a fair amount of property advertising. Once again, there's no way you will be able to buy the property without going to see it but do make sure you arrange to see a good range of property before making a special trip. If at all possible, try and get the sellers to send you as many photographs as they can of the property. If they are unable to do this, it's worth wondering why.

You will find that the people promoting Portuguese property in the UK fall into three categories:

1   There are independent agents who may represent a range of builders or developers in Portugal (and also private purchasers) and any one developer may negotiate terms with a range of independent agents.
2   Estate agents in this country have expanded into Europe and provide a similar service to that which they provide in the UK.
3   The Portuguese developers themselves may have set up sales outlets in the UK and promote their own properties on their own behalf.

Portuguese estate agents

Estate agents in Portugal are registered as such and hold a Government licence which permits them to sell property. Their publicity should make it clear that they are registered and that they have the necessary licences. This licence merely gives them the authority to sell property – it is of course no guarantee that the estate agent is reputable or trustworthy. That is up to you to find out for yourself and you should of course be aware that estate agents in Portugal are not bound by any kind of consumer protection laws.

There are trade associations of estate agents (in Lisbon and Oporto) but these are mainly set up to protect the agents themselves against developers who may at times be reluctant to pay the agreed levels of commission.

Most of the estate agents will of course work perfectly ethically but there is probably a greater tendency than in the UK for estate agents to be less independent and to represent either their own projects or those where they have a sole agency agreement with a developer. In cases like these, the prices may be under the estate agent's control, ie he has an agreement with the owner to sell at a certain price and anything over and above that price is commission. In some cases, agents may purchase property themselves for the purposes of re-sale and, provided they do so within two years of purchase, they are exempt from purchase tax. Obviously, by acquiring the property direct from the owners and sorting out any problems on title, they are then in a position to sell the property at a handsome profit.

Although you won't find as many estate agents in the Portuguese high street as you will at home, there are a number of organisations that will be offering property for sale (both new and second-hand) and most of them will have somebody who can speak English. If you have taken the trouble to go to Portugal and look for yourself, it can be very worthwhile just wandering up and down the main street of the local town looking for the *mediador autorizado* (literally 'authorised mediator') and doing exactly what you do in England – ie compare prices.

Seeing for yourself

Sooner or later, though, you are going to have to take the plunge and go out to Portugal and see for yourself. It is folly to buy property that you have not seen (some people do, believe it or not) and it's no good relying on memories of a two week holiday on which to base your decision on where to live in Portugal. You have got to go out and see for yourself and preferably at a time when it might not be looking at its most glamorous. You will find that many developers and agents will lay on long weekends and some of them will offer you the opportunity to travel free and also put you up in a hotel at their expense. On the other hand, the only properties you are going to see by this route are those that the developer has on offer but it can be an inexpensive way of seeing a particular area. Some developers aren't quite this generous; they make you pay, with the incentive that they will refund the costs if you sign on the dotted line. On balance, it's probably better to pay the bill and sign on the dotted line when it suits you, not the developer.

Arranging a visit yourself

These long weekends are a good opportunity to have a look around but why not be a little more courageous and make the trip under your own steam? If you are thinking of spending many thousands of pounds on a property in Portugal, it really does make a lot of sense to spend some time looking at all the opportunities open to you. It is, of course, very straightforward to do this – any travel agent will be able to fix you up with a flight, inexpensive hotel accommodation and a hire car and you will find that rates in the autumn and winter are not at all expensive.

Do take the time to look around properly. If you are going to move into an area you will need to know as much about it as you would about a new area in the UK. The one thing that most popular areas in Portugal aren't short of is fellow countrymen so you can always find somebody to talk to in a restaurant or bar who will be more than pleased to give you as much information as you are likely to be able to absorb in a week!

What can you legally buy?

The Portuguese authorities are, in principle, enthusiastic about foreigners buying property and becoming 'permanent tourists'. On the other hand, they are determined to keep a close eye on all building development to make sure that it doesn't get out of control.

For this purpose, they've established a set of rules for foreigners buying property and in the rules they make some distinctions between tourists and residents.

As a resident, you have the right to purchase more than one house, if you have residence permit of classification A (ie the type that is renewed annually). If you have residence permit B (which can only be issued after you have been resident in Portugal for five years and which is issued for five years) then you are also free from the restrictions on buying large plots of farmland (you will find full details of residence qualifications in chapter 15).

As a tourist you may only buy one holiday home (or the plot on which to build it) for your family and, **in general**, the size of the plot must not exceed 5,000 square metres. (If you wish to buy a plot of more than 5,000 square metres you should get professional advice from your lawyer.) Clearly, this is a very large plot and in an urbanisation it would be significantly smaller than this, in the region of 1,000 square metres (but see the section on buying agricultural land). If you wish to buy more than one property, the additional properties must be for investment purposes only and they must be on an urbanisation. This means, for example, that you would not be able to buy two plots of land or a holiday home and a *quinta* (a farmhouse).

Purchase of a property through a company

The impact of inheritance tax and capital gains tax (see chapter 13) can be severe on the foreign property owner. It could therefore be very worth your while to consider setting up a company outside Portugal with the sole purpose of purchasing property in Portugal. The Bank of Portugal allows this to be done provided the company is set up for the purpose of providing a holiday home for its directors.

This is how it is done:

- You will first of all need to set up the company. This could be done in the UK or it could alternatively be done off shore (ie in the Isle of Man or the Channel Islands). It is of course important that the company is correctly 'serviced'. It will be necessary to appoint directors, and to hold annual general meetings in the usual way. Annual returns must be filed each year with the Companies Registry and, unless the company has an exempt status, audited accounts must also be submitted to the local income tax office. It is likely that the cost of running such a company in the Channel Islands could be up to as much as £1,000 a year depending on the degree of professional help you need (although the costs of an Isle of Man company could be lower). Failure to run the company properly could result in it being struck off with serious consequences, particularly if the company was the owner of Portuguese property.
- You must obtain a tax card (a *cartao de pessoa colectiva*) for the company from the local tax department. You will need:

  — a copy of the certificate of incorporation
  — a copy of the main objects of the company
  — details of the registered office.

- The company must give power of attorney (translated into

Portuguese) to a person nominated by it to sign on its behalf.

Apart from supplying one or two extra documents as outlined above, and obtaining a different tax card, purchasing a property through a company is no different from buying it in your own name. The advantage from the taxation point of view is that the company owns the property and the property is unaffected by changes in the ownership (either by death or by sale of the company to other individuals). Overall, the tax liability can be substantially reduced by using a company to buy property with the one important proviso that tax **is** payable if one shareholder acquires 75% or more of the company's share capital.

It is strongly recommended that you get competent professional advice before undertaking this method of property purchase.

Basic things to check when buying property

When you are buying any property (including land), you will need to know that the person selling it has good title to it, ie that he is in a position to sell it. You will need to know the full address of the property and the land registry description of the property as well as all the inscriptions (ie who actually is the registered owner) which you will find in the land registry in the area in which the property is situated. You will also need a legalised copy of the seller's *escritura* (the title deed to the property) to ensure that there are no restrictions on the use of the property or any other covenants which the seller entered into and which would be binding on you. You should then get your lawyer to apply for a full search on the property (known as a *certidao de teor*) to make sure that the seller is the registered owner of the property

and that there are no mortgages or other charges registered
against it.

You will find full details of the legal process in chapter 7.

Do not forget to make a search at the tax department to make
sure that the rates have been paid and are up to date.

In addition to ensuring that the seller has good title, you
should also obtain a copy of the *caderneta predial* (which is
issued by the local tax office in the area in which the property
is situated) or a search, also known as a *certidao de teor* and
check this closely with the land registry details. You should
also obtain a copy of the habitation certificate if the property
was built after 1951.

Finally, you should ask for copies of the last receipts for
electricity and water and also the last receipt for the local rates.
You should only pay a small deposit on account of the price
agreed, pointing out in writing at the time that the sale is
on condition that all payments, taxes and charges are kept
up-to-date until the day the property is transferred to you.

A newly built property will normally have been built with
better materials and under new and stricter building
regulations. Naturally, you are not going to get any choice in
the finish or in the fixtures and fittings. Also a house that
has been built speculatively may be rather more expensive
because the developer is going to include in the price the
costs of financing the construction and some element of
compensation for the risks he is running by building
speculatively in the first place.

When you buy a newly built property, it is essential to find
out whether a certificate of habitation has been issued. If
not, you should enquire when it is likely to be available
because without it you will not be able to get your title to
the property. The existence of the certificate will also be
evidence that the property has been built in accordance with
the local planning rules for the area. You also need to check

that it is connected (or will ultimately be connected) to all
the local services according to the plans from the point of
view of roads, water supply, electricity supply and sewerage.
In any case, you would be well advised to check with the
water company and the electricity company that the services
are available and also ask them to confirm in writing that the
services will be provided when you or the builder supplies
them with the necessary documents.

Buying a property in the planning stage or under development
will usually be at a lower price than a newly built house and
you can sometimes have some of your own ideas incorporated
in the construction. As with any kind of building work, you
should always make sure you are purchasing from solid
companies and only pay according to the development of the
work, **never** in advance (although you might have to make
an initial payment to cover the cost of materials).

Buying a house under construction is a little more
complicated. You should ask to see a copy of the building
licence and the payment slip for it, and check out the
guarantees for the completion of the infrastructure ie the
roads, water supply and electricity supply.

6 Buying land and building new property

Introduction

If you are really adventurous you can buy a plot of land and build your house on it. Naturally, the legal niceties should be taken care of in connection with the house construction (see chapter 7) but, in addition, you will need to know a lot more about the land itself. Never assume that just because land is for sale it can automatically be built on.

When you are buying land with the intention of building a property on it you have four basic stages to go through:

1 You have to buy the land.
2 Planning permission has to be obtained from the local authority.
3 Plans have to be drawn up with an architect.
4 You will need a firm contract with the builder.

Chapter 7 covers the contractual and legal aspects of house purchase – this chapter will concentrate on dealing with the Town Hall and finding your way around the planning rules, together with the things to bear in mind when designing and building a house to your own specification.

Much of this chapter will deal specifically with building your own house but even if you are buying from a developer you cannot assume that the planning aspects have been correctly dealt with. You should always ask for evidence that the property is being built in accordance with the planning rules – which in Portugal are getting tighter all the time.

Buying a plot

The checks to make

If you wish to buy a plot, the first thing you must discover is what sort of classification it has been given by the Land Registry. If it is part of what is known as a *loteamento* which will be registered at the Land Registry, the land itself will have already been designated for building purposes. If the land is merely registered as rustic land, then you need to be aware of the restrictions on a foreigner buying land and local planning rules (see later).

Checks on agricultural land

If you want to build on an agricultural plot, then you have other enquiries to make. You must also make sure that you will get water, electricity, road access and (eventually) the telephone if you want it. Don't trust verbal assurances, make sure to get it in writing. Only the questions you ask will be answered so take nothing for granted and work out your questions carefully.

It's not unusual to have to rely on your own well for water so have a test boring made to determine the amount and quality of the water. If you are intending to link up with a main water supply, be sure to find out whether this will be allowed and whether you will be granted permission to lay a pipe on other people's property that has to be crossed.

The electricity line near to, or crossing your land may not be at the right voltage and you may or may not be permitted to make a direct connection to it. It's essential to consult the local electricity company not only for permission but also to find out about the costs of any transformers, poles and transmission lines that may be needed.

To build access roads to more important roads, you need

permission from the authorities. If you have to cross other people's property, you need their written consent. There may be a road nearby that you are planning to use for access. But check first – is it really a public road or is it a private one?

Check the title

Before you start the negotiations to buy the land, you need to know whether the seller has got good legal title to it and whether or not you will get permission to build on it. The seller may say that the land is not agricultural, but merely rustic land (which means that you should be able to build on it). You should make sure. You should first visit the local tax office to find out if the land is registered there and whether there is any information you can find out about it. If the land is being sold on the basis that planning permission has been granted, then you can find out from the Town Hall if an application has been made and whether it has been granted.

If the land is not registered in the Land Registry or at the tax office, then you need to tread carefully in your subsequent negotiations. Somebody is going to have to examine a lot of records to find out if the seller has got good title to the land and this could mean going back over several years and looking for a lot of people if the land has been passed down from generation to generation.

The planning rules

At one time, building property in Portugal was a very casual affair with little attention being paid to local planning rules. That is no longer the case and you'll find that the planning regulations in Portugal are gradually becoming as tight as they are in the UK. The authorities are now realising that badly designed and illegal developments can quickly become substandard and detract from the area as a whole and so they are now getting much tighter in the way they control building. There's no particular problem in this as far as the property buyer is concerned – it just means that you need to take more care than you might have had to some time ago. It's therefore important when considering building property that you make sure that you apply for planning permission and that if you're buying a partially built house, the builder has obtained planning permission as well.

You should also bear in mind that there is no one set of planning rules that is common to Portugal. You will find that there are local variations that will arise according to the specific needs of different local authorities. For example, some local authorities will require you to obtain permission from the department within the Ministry of Agriculture dealing with *ambiente* in the area. The nearest equivalent in the UK is of obtaining permission to build on a green belt area or in an 'area of outstanding natural beauty'.

Most local authorities have separate planning departments staffed with architects, engineers and other professional staff. They ensure that the planning regulations are adhered to and that buildings are not built haphazardly so as to spoil the area. If you are buying a plot in a development which has planning permission, the local authority will have demanded financial guarantees from developers in order to ensure that they put in adequate and satisfactory infrastructures (eg that the roads are wide enough for traffic, that they are able to withstand the heat and occasional torrential rain, that the water pipes can supply the water that's required in the peak season and that the sewage disposal system works).

In some areas, you may find that the planning regulations aren't quite so tight but that's not a reason for congratulation. You may subsequently find that another developer has started to build in front of your property completely blocking your view.

It's therefore important if you're considering building new property to investigate the planning regulations thoroughly and

to find out just how tight they are. If they don't seem tight
at all, then that may be good reason for building your property
somewhere else.

It will help you if you engage a lawyer or a registered real
estate agent to assist you with the legal searches before
committing yourself. You might also find that you need the
assistance of a land surveyor as well to define the boundaries
and size of the plot. Don't forget, the *mais ou menos* attitude
may well apply to the plot you intend to buy. The last thing
you want to do is to commit yourself to buying something
only to find that the boundaries are not where you thought
they were.

The planning system

The planning system in Portugal is relatively straightforward
but the diagram on the following page will explain the steps
you have to go through. Each step is then explained in more
detail in the succeeding paragraphs.

Restrictions on foreigners buying land – Decree Law 38/86

Decree Law 38/86 introduced the rule that foreigners cannot
purchase more than 5,000m^2 of 'agricultural' land (ie rustic
land which has an agricultural purpose and is included in the
national reserve) unless permission is given to them by the
Institute of Foreign Investment which is based in Lisbon and
Oporto and is the body which authorises inward investment
into Portugal. (From some time in 1989, the Institute of
Foreign Investment will be disbanded and permission to
acquire agricultural land will be given by the Bank of
Portugal.) However, the rule only applies to land which has
an agricultural purpose and not to unproductive land. Where
land is unproductive the general rule is that you can apply

to purchase an area of land not exceeding the 'unit of agriculture' established for your area and submit your application for an import licence to the Bank of Portugal in the normal way.

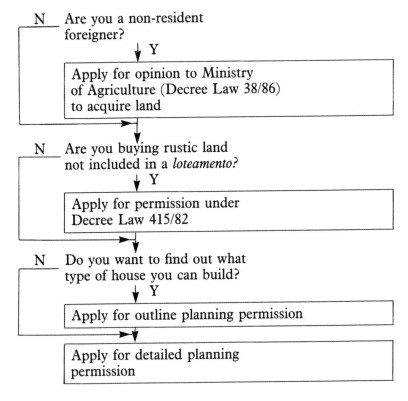

You will have to obtain an 'opinion' from the local office of the Ministry of Agriculture in your district the (*Direccao Regional de Agricultura*) as to the condition of the land and whether it has any agricultural use. This opinion has to be submitted to the Bank of Portugal in accordance with *Decree Law 38/86* together with the other documents which are necessary to obtain an import licence for the money to purchase the land (see chapter 8). You will need to make a request to the Regional Director of Agriculture and enclose the following documents:

- Two copies of the map of the general area on a scale of 1:25,000.
- Two copies of the map of your plot on a scale not inferior to 1:2,000
- Documentary proof that the plot has been registered in the tax department.
- A short statement as to the type of building you propose to erect on the plot you want to buy.
- A photocopy of the promissory contract of purchase and sale.

If you wish to purchase a plot of land which has a productive use and is over 5,000m² you will have to make an application to the Bank of Portugal. Permission will not be given if you cannot show that you will use the land productively, ie farm it, and that you yourself have some knowledge of agriculture.

If you are an EEC national resident within the EEC then the method of application is by what is known as 'previous declaration'. You will need to obtain the appropriate forms from the Bank of Portugal or from the Portuguese Chamber of Commerce in the UK who generally have a stock of them. Fill them in carefully and submit the application with the following documents:

- A copy of the promissory contract of purchase and sale of the land.
- A letter from your local authority in the UK confirming that you are on the register of electors.
- Photocopies of the first four pages of your passport.
- Documents stating that you are a farmer, experienced market gardener etc.

It is generally thought best to use a lawyer or other professional person who is used to dealing with the Bank of Portugal to handle the application on your behalf. Provided all the correct documents are submitted in the proper manner, then the Bank is duty bound to give you a reply within 60 days. If they do not, then the application is tacitly approved. The approval from the Bank comes in the form of a letter written to the applicant stating the conditions on which the investment is to be made.

You must give the notary a copy of your permission from the Bank otherwise he will not transfer the title of the land to you. The permission given by the Bank is valid for a period of 90 days in which time you must complete all the formalities of your purchase (but, if there is a delay, you may apply for renewal of the permission which is generally granted).

Getting planning permission

Permission to build a house is obtained from the local Town Hall (the *Camara*) in the area in which your property is situated. Initially, it is probably worthwhile visiting the Town Hall yourself informally and getting hold of the official in charge of granting planning permits to make sure that they are basically in favour of granting permission for your particular house.

Planning permission on rustic land – Decree Law 451/82

If you intend applying for planning permission on **rustic** land you will initially need approval from the local office of the Ministry of Agriculture in your district (the *Direccao Regional de Agricultura*) under *Decree Law 451/82*. From the Town Hall you will need three copies of a map of your plot (scale 1:10,000) and three copies of a map of the general area (scale 1:25,000), indicating the site. On these must be marked the boundaries of the land and the exact site of the house that you intend to build. You then send the maps, plus a request (in Portuguese) on official paper, to the Ministry asking them for their opinion (and be prepared to wait some time for the answer).

Outline planning permission

You can, however, make an official request to the local authority asking them whether in principle they will be prepared to allow you to build on the plot concerned. This application is known as *Viabilidade de Construcao sem Proposta* (which roughly means 'Viability of a Construction without Proposal' ie outline planning permission). In order to obtain this you will need to make a request on official paper and enclose the opinion that you obtained from the local Ministry of Agriculture. You will also need a map of your plot (scale 1:2,000) on which you have outlined the boundaries and the exact position of the house that you intend to build and a map of the area (scale 1:25,000) on which you have marked your plot. The maps must be authenticated by the local authority and all the documents must be submitted in triplicate.

If you want to obtain outline planning permission for a particular type of building and/or requesting permission for however many square metres of constructed area, then you will need to have the support of the owner of the property. He (or his attorney) must sign the official request enclosing all the documents stated above, in triplicate, and adding documentary proof of ownership of the plot.

The advantage of obtaining outline planning permission is that you at least have some sort of indication that you will be able to build on the plot which you are buying so when you come to apply for detailed planning permission, it will be granted more quickly.

Detailed planning permission

Obtaining detailed planning permission is best left to your architect who will have to draw up plans for the house, list the building materials he is going to use, deal with the question of infrastructures and so on. The actual application for planning permission will be made in your name and you will have to sign the official request or give someone a power of attorney to do it on your behalf.

If you are building on rustic land, you will have applied for an opinion from the Ministry. When you receive this approval then it's back to the Town Hall who will also want to see the maps of the area, the plot and the proposed site of the building on the plot. They will want to see the letter of approval from the Ministry and an official request from you (in Portuguese) explaining exactly the purpose of the building. If you are a tourist, it should be for a 'holiday home'; if you've become a resident, then you should write for 'permanent residence'. You can then expect another waiting period (unless the planning consent is refused) after which you will be able to obtain the building permit (the *alvara*). If the Town Hall has not replied within 60 days, permission is tacitly approved. You can then start concentrating on the builder and the architect.

Dealing with the developer

On your very first meeting with the developer (and this may even happen when you have your first meeting with the sales agent) you may be asked to sign a piece of paper 'to reserve the house for you'. This is generally to put you under some kind of obligation and there is usually no need to sign anything. However, in some cases, you may prefer to go back to the UK knowing that you have some kind of hold over the property that took your fancy. However, do be sure that you know exactly what you are signing. A reservation is simply to reserve a plot or property for, say, two weeks while you make up your mind. There should be no need to pay over any money but if you do, make sure that it is returnable in full if you decide not to go ahead. You may not have any legal redress if things go wrong. At the same time, make sure the reservation you sign is just that and not a contract to purchase in disguise (it has been known!). Don't sign anything that is only in Portuguese – insist on a translation.

The buying process

There are two ways in which you can buy a new property from a developer:

1   You can buy one ready built or one that is in course of construction (in which case you need to be clear about planning permission ie that the developer is permitted to build the house he wishes to sell you).
2   You can buy a plot of land and have a dwelling built on it.

In either case, you will need a good contract with the developer and you also need to be sure that, when the house is completed, you will get access to services you need (roads, water, electricity,) and that the property (when it is finished) has been correctly constructed and is fit to live in.

If the house is partially constructed, the developer will offer you a contract for the finished product. If the house is not yet started, then you should insist on buying the land first. In the latter case, you may find that the developer (if he is the owner of the land) may also ask you to sign an exclusive contract for the construction of the property as well. This clearly restricts your freedom of action but it's not entirely unreasonable.

Some developers will often propose in their contracts that you will only get title to the property when all the money has been paid over (ie both for the plot and for the construction). This is really quite dangerous because you would not have any legal protection at all for the money that you've paid out if the developer goes into liquidation while the house is being built (and that is not at all unknown). What you should ensure is that the building contract contains a clause which stipulates that no building work will take place and no payments for any building work will be made until you get title to the land. It would not also be unreasonable to insist that construction work starts within a reasonable period of the land becoming yours, eg within, say two months.

The other reason for having a separate contract is purely financial. If the plot belongs to the developer, then this may be used as a lever to request additional payment for the construction (ie over and above the agreed price) and you may have difficulty getting all the necessary documents when construction is complete unless you make these extra payments. If you own the plot, then the developer has no lever for demanding extra payment (although he does, of course, have the full backing of the law in getting you to pay the agreed price for the construction or to pay additional amounts if you have asked for alterations).

Dealing with the architect

If you're going to build a property from scratch and you have a plot in mind, your first task is to select an architect and sit down and discuss in detail the potential house plans with him. It's important for you because you might be living in the property for some time and it's important for him because he's going to send you a bill of around 10% of the building costs. For that type of expenditure, you are entitled to expect time and commitment from him both in preparation of the plans and also in controlling the building of the property.

It is also recommended that you get hold of an architect before you buy the land. You should give him a sketch of the house you want to build and indicate the position on the plot where you would like it to be built. This is useful because not only will it tell you whether or not the house that you want is capable of being built on the plot but it will also ensure that the proposals that you submit to the Town Hall will be final

– if you move the position of the house on the site after permission has been granted, you may then find yourself with some problems.

The sort of things that you should discuss with the architect could contain some items which you are not entirely familiar with having been used to living in the UK.

Go to the plot and discuss the siting of the house with the architect. Portugal can be quite hilly – and it's not at all unusual to have to build a house on sloping ground (and in any subsequent quotations check the cost of the foundations and any retaining walls).

Work out what the views will be. Much of life in Portugal is spent sitting on terraces in the sunshine – you need to know what you're going to be looking at.

You will need to be able to protect your house (and yourself) against the fierce heat of the sun in summer but you also want to get as much sun into the house as possible in the winter.

Don't forget that you probably intend to spend a fair bit of time outside your home, perhaps sitting on a terrace. Is there room for a terrace? Does it have adequate illumination? Is the terrace sheltered from the prevailing winds (which can blow with some force in the coastal areas)?

Think about how much space you and your family will need not only today but in the years to come. Your home may be built for holidays but even on holiday you need wardrobes and cupboard space. Even though you may not plan to spend much time in the kitchen, remember that you are probably going to want a breakfast and so a reasonable size of kitchen area could be a blessing.

You will need to avoid steep and narrow stairs if you are infirm or getting on in years.

Find ways of diverting water away from the house when it rains (because when it rains in Portugal, it can be very heavy indeed).

Try to make as much use as possible of traditional building styles and local materials.

Consider the possibility of using solar heating, collecting rainwater for watering the garden and the recycling of grey water (ie bath water).

Think about heating the house in winter and make sure that you have a fireplace that works.

Think about keeping the house cool in summer and work out the airflow through the house (ie getting a cool breeze flowing through the bedrooms).

Think about having an extra water tank (a *cisterna*) installed.

In parts of Portugal, hard water can be a problem. You might find a water softener would be useful.

Think carefully about the siting of light fittings, switches and electrical power points both inside and outside the house.

Take into consideration the height of working surfaces both in the kitchens and bathrooms. Portuguese people tend, on average, to be slightly shorter than people from the UK and they tend in some cases to site their working surfaces slightly lower than we are used to.

Think about the security of your house and put iron grilles on all external doors and windows and consider installing a safe. Make sure your doors are strong.

And don't forget the greatest problem in many Portuguese houses is insulation against water, heat and cold. It's not unusual to find houses built into hillsides and also built on rock. The water flow down a rocky hillside can be quite substantial and the last thing you need is areas in the construction where water can be trapped. If you have a roof terrace make sure that it's well insulated against water penetration. All your terraces should slope well away from the house. Try and ensure that you have roof overhangs to protect windows and doors.

The summers can be hot – and sun coming through a large window can make the inside of a house like a furnace. Consider having blinds built into the window constructions and don't forget to think about mosquito netting. There's nothing worse on a hot summer's night than being unable to open the windows to let in some cool air because of the invasion by insects.

The winters can be damp and cold on the Portuguese coast. Having well insulated walls may seem like something you only need to think about in the UK – it's something to think about in Portugal as well.

The final point, of course, is to make sure that you can afford to build the house that your architect intends to design. Before he undertakes the detailed design work, ask for an estimate of the likely cost of the property so that you can trim back the plans if they turn out to be a little over-ambitious. Once you've agreed with your architect what the plan should be, you then need to ask him to prepare a full description of building materials and this together with the plan forms an integral part of the building contract.

The building contract

Preliminary matters

The sort of details that the contract should cover are as follows:

- It should contain the name and address of the builder. If it is a company, then the place and the date of registration should be given as well together with the authority of the person signing the contract.
- It should clearly identify the property.
- It should state that the construction will be on the basis of the plans of the architect (and you should ensure that the plans and the schedule of building quantities and qualities are signed by the architect and included as part of the contract).
- It should specify the size of the house (in square metres). Make sure the figure relates to **living space**. Occasionally

you may find that it includes the terrace, solarium etc
which is misleading.
- It must specify the total price and also what is and what
  is not included in the total price such as:

  — Service connections
  — Retaining walls
  — Entrance drive
  — Landscaping
  — Swimming pool with machinery
  — Fireplace
  — Exterior stairs and rails
  — Window grilles
  — Lamps
  — Kitchen equipment
  — Bathroom equipment
  — Solar heating installation
  — Additional water storage tank etc.

- It should contain an agreed date by which the building
  should be finished and should also (if relevant) indicate
  a date by which the work will be started. There should
  also be a clause incorporating a penalty for the builder
  to pay if the property is not finished in time.
- It would be normal to pay a certain percentage of the total
  building price in advance so that the builder can buy
  materials (but this should not be more than, say, 30% of
  the total).
- It should contain a schedule of payments according to the
  phase of construction and not fixed dates. The money
  stipulated for each phase should be paid against
  certificates supplied by the architect (and don't forget
  you need an import licence to cover all your payments –
  see chapter 8).
- The builder may insist on a clause to charge you interest
  if the payments are late.
- There should be a clause covering the remedying of any
  defects you discover after you have taken possession of
  the property.
- There should be a clause indicating that at the same time

as the final payment, the keys will be handed over
together with the certificate of habitation. You may then
immediately arrange for the registration of the property
at the land registry.
- The contract should specify whether or not the price
  includes any taxes, the cost of the building licence etc.

Possible problems

There has been a tendency in the Algarve primarily among
the foreign builders to write building contracts on the back
of a postage stamp! These contracts may have just perhaps
two or three clauses stating the price of the house, when
stage payments are due and what penalty you will have to pay
the builder if you are late in making your stage payments.
If you are faced with one of these contracts and are told that
the builder will not renegotiate his terms then you should
think very carefully before using his services. Sometimes you
will be put in an impossible situation if he sold you the land
himself and included in the contract of purchase for the land
a clause stating that he will undertake the building work
which will have to be started in a certain period of time. If
you are in this position, then the following suggestions may
be helpful.

Builders all over the world have a reputation for being
difficult, slow and never finishing on time (which is not **always**
deserved provided you choose your builder with care). At the
end of the day, of course, the value of any contract depends
entirely on whether you can sue on it successfully.
Consequently, even if you have the most tightly drawn up
contract, it will not be of much use to you if the builder
himself is so under capitalised that he would not be able to
pay damages awarded for breach of contract. The first thing
therefore is to make sure that your builder is financially
sound and that any work he has done previously has been
satisfactorily carried out. This you can find out by making
enquiries at his bank and asking other purchasers on the
development whether they are happy with his work. If he is

a freelance builder then you should ask him to show you a house that he has built recently and then talk to the owners.

Ask for prices from more than one reputable builder (your architect will help you here). Check that you are actually contracting with the builder himself and not with the middle-man (occasionally, some people make building contracts with clients as if they were the real builders and then sub-contract the building to another builder).

In reality, while you may have a good idea of what you want in the contract your builder may have other ideas and will ask you to accept his contract. In this case you must insist that at least two further clauses be inserted into the contract, if they are not there already. The first should state when the building work is going to start (adding, hopefully, when it is to be finished!) The second should state that all matters that have not been dealt with in the contract should be governed by the appropriate provisions in the Portuguese Civil Code. The effect of this clause will be to make the builder concentrate on the matter in hand! If your builder is not prepared to accept this clause then you should consider looking elsewhere because he may be unlikely to uphold your statutory rights.

Building contracts under the Portuguese Civil Code 1966

The building contract (known as *empreitada*) is provided for specifically in the Civil Code under articles 1,207 to 1,230 inclusive. The Code gives you the following protection.

As owner of the land, you acquire ownership of the construction as and when it is built irrespective of whether or not the builders supplied the materials. Materials supplied must be at least of average quality and you may periodically check the progress of the building in order to ascertain that the correct materials are being used, and that generally all is well (providing you do so at your own expense and do not disturb the builders working). The building must be constructed in accordance with an agreed plan which may not be altered in any way without your consent.

The price which is stated in the contract is a fixed price and cannot be increased by the builder (unless, of course, additional work has been required for technical reasons or at your request). If the builder starts asking for more money, you should seek legal advice before agreeing to pay anything. You are, however, entitled to make certain alterations to the plan providing that the value of these does not exceed one-fifth of the stipulated price and that you are not changing the nature of the work. If these changes result in the builder having to do extra work then he will, of course, be entitled to be paid for this as well as being given extra time to complete the building. However if your changes result in the builder having to do less work, you may in certain circumstances be entitled to a reduction in the original price.

When the builder communicates to you that he has finished the building then you are allowed a reasonable time to go and inspect it. If you are not able to go out to Portugal and inspect the building yourself then it would be worthwhile to employ a professional to do so on your behalf. If you fail to arrange for the building to be inspected then you will be deemed to have accepted the building work as it is.

After the property has been accepted, you must give the builder a list of all the things which are wrong within 30 days of your discovering them. You are then entitled to make the builder put everything right or to ask for a reduction in the price. However, in respect of all the defects that are known to you, you must exercise your rights in respect of them within a year of their discovery. As to the defects that were unknown to you (and necessarily of a nature where you could not possibly have known about them), then the year runs from the date on which you discover them. However, no claims can be made after **two years** from the date of the acceptance of the building.

A builder is also required to put right any structural defects within a period of five years starting from the date when you have officially accepted the property.

It is obvious from the above that the more 'enlightened' builders want purchasers to sign contracts which restrict their rights under the Portuguese Civil Code. For example, since the Code allows you a reasonable time to go and inspect a property and as the likelihood is that you will do so normally towards the end of the building (after all you will want to see your new home), the builder will seek to pin you down to a particular date so that he can engineer your acceptance of the building.

On the other hand it is up to you to negotiate a contract to your best advantage but you need to seek professional advice. It will help your lawyer if you sit down with your builder and get him to agree with you the detailed specifications which you should both then initial.

Penalties for late completion

Needless to say, most builders will strongly resist any form of penalty on them in the event that they fail to complete the building on time. However, builders are indeed getting more used to accepting that they have to use their very best endeavours to meet their contractual obligations. Penalties are generally fixed by reference to a daily rate or to a percentage of the outstanding work at the end of a contract.

The documents on completion of construction

When the house is completed, you will not be able officially to move into your home until it has been inspected by a representative from the Town Hall. Following this inspection, your house will be given a certificate of habitation (without which you cannot get your property connected to the electricity supply) after which you are free to take up occupation.

You now have everything you need to take up occupation of your house and the next stage is to take the certificate of habitation to the Land Registry and to the tax office and get the property registered for rates. The tax office will provide you with a *caderneta predial* and the land registry will provide you with the land registration certificate.

7 Understanding the legalities

Finding a lawyer

You will probably be able to find an English speaking lawyer (an *advogado*) in most of the main tourist centres in Portugal but an alternative is to go to your solicitor in the UK and ask him to recommend a firm of solicitors who deal with overseas property transactions. You could also contact the Law Society who keep a register of Portuguese lawyers practising in the UK as well as firms of solicitors specialising in this field.

When buying property in the UK, you can expect your solicitor to undertake all of the necessary legal work involved in conveyancing property and you may well have means of redress if he fails to do the job properly. No such means exist **in the UK** for taking action against a Portuguese lawyer. If you have any problems subsequently, you may find it difficult to obtain redress or to get the problem sorted out. To some extent, therefore, there are some advantages in using a London based lawyer attached to a UK firm of solicitors because they at least will operate in a way which is more in keeping with UK standards. Nevertheless, it still pays to make quite sure that you and he understand exactly what you expect him to do. Your lawyer will of course advise you on what should be done – and you should listen carefully to what he has to suggest.

The ten steps to property purchase

What follows is a summary of the process that you as a new property buyer will have to go through when buying property in Portugal.

1   You may start with a reservation **possibly** paying out a small (and preferably refundable) deposit.
2   You then ask your lawyer to do the necessary searches in the local land registry to see:

- Who is the owner of the property.
- Is his title good?
- Does the description of the property tie up with the property you hope to buy?
- Are there any mortgages or other charges on the property?
- Does any other person have any interest in the property?

In addition to examining the *escritura* to see if there are any restrictive covenants, your lawyer should also go to the local tax office (the *reparticao de financas*) where the property is registered to check in whose name the property is registered and (if buying land) that the registered area corresponds to that registered at the local land registry (otherwise, there will be problems later on with the *escritura*).

3   If it's a new building, you should go to the Town Hall to find out that whatever has been built has all the necessary licences and permits and to make sure that no new planning rules will affect it.
4   You should go to the local tax office to make sure that the seller has paid all the taxes due on the property up to the point of sale.
5   Provided your lawyer is happy that the seller has good title to the property, you may now sign the purchasing contract (*contrato de promessa de compra e venda*) which is

legally binding and commits you to the purchase and the vendor to the sale.

6 Your next stage is to apply for the import licence for foreign currency (the *boletim de autorizacao de importacao de capitais privados* – see chapter 8) and apply for your tax card from the local tax office (see Form A).

7 You must then pay the *Sisa* (see chapter 13) or obtain a certificate of exemption from the local tax office.

8 With the import licence, you can now arrange for the *escritura* to be made which transfers ownership of the property to you.

9 The *escritura* is then taken to the local land registry (*conservatoria do registo predial*) to be registered.

10 Finally, you register with the local tax office for paying local rates either amending the *caderneta predial* or obtaining a new one.

After all the above has been satisfactorily concluded, you should have in your hand the following documents:

• The contract.
• The import licence for the currency.
• A receipt for payment of *Sisa* (if required) or exemption certificate if appropriate.
• Your legalised copy of the *escritura*.
• A certificate from the local land registry that your property is correctly registered there.
• Your tax card from the *reparticao de financas* identifying you as a local taxpayer.
• A *caderneta predial* made out to you by the *reparticao de financas*.

The legal process

The two key stages in the purchase of property in Portugal are:

1 The contract of purchase and sale.
2 The conveyancing of the property.

A—Application for tax card

Modelo n.° Fiscal do Contribuinte — P. Singular (n.° 1/NI da D. G. C. I.)

MINISTÉRIO DAS FINANÇAS E DO PLANO
Direcção-Geral das Contribuições e Impostos
NÚMERO FISCAL DO CONTRIBUINTE — PESSOA SINGULAR
FICHA DE INSCRIÇÃO — Original

IMPORTANTE: Leia as instruções no verso do duplicado antes de iniciar o preenchimento da ficha.

Número de Ficha de Inscrição

c 1 6 1 1 6 9 3 5

2 Nome completo

3 Domicílio Fiscal   3.1 Rua, Avenida, etc.
3.2 Número ou Lote   3.3 Andar, Plano, etc.
3.4 Localidade
3.5 Freguesia
3.6 Código postal

4 Local de nascimento
4.1 Freguesia
4.2 Concelho
4.3 Distrito ou País

6 Data de nascimento
Dia   Mês   Ano

7 Sexo
Masculino 1   Feminino 2

8 Nacionalidade
Portuguesa 1   Outra 2

5 Descrição profissional
5.1
5.2
5.3

9 Estado Civil
Casado 1   Solteiro, etc. 2
10 Bilhete de Identidade
Número   Arquivo

Declaro ser esta a primeira inscrição que faço para efeitos da atribuição do Número Fiscal do Contribuinte — Pessoa Singular, e que as declarações nela expressas correspondem à verdade sem qualquer omissão em relação às mesmas

Local e data
Assinatura

O .... procurador, gestor de negócios, etc.
N.° Fiscal ou do B. I. do procurador, gestor de negócios, etc.   Arquivo

11 N.° Fiscal do Cônjuge
Seg. judicial solteiro, etc. 2

Obs.:

Válido até ____/____/____

Assinatura do Recebente

CARIMBO DO RECEPTOR

Modelo n.° 925 (Exclusivo da INCM)

Both these stages are vitally important to the property owner. However, in Portugal there are a number of different types of property ownership:

- In the first case, of course, you can become the outright owner of a property (eg a villa) with your own pool, garden and so on.
- As an alternative, you could share the legal ownership of the property with other members of your family or friends ie co-ownership.
- You may choose to buy an apartment where, in addition, you own a share of various common areas, eg the gardens, pool etc. This type of ownership is covered by the law of horizontal property.
- You may decide to buy a timeshare ie you buy the right to use a property for a stated period during the year.

Timesharing has its own special legal environment and this is covered in detail in chapter 10. The bulk of this chapter will cover the arrangements for buying any privately owned property and at the end of the chapter we look at the special situations of co-ownership and the ownership of apartments.

The search

One of the most fundamental aspects of buying property in Portugal is that the ownership of land is all important. Whoever owns the land owns what is built on it. Consequently, ownership of land is very important in the Portuguese system and land is often used as security to cover mortgages and other debts. Until the debt is repaid, it becomes a completely integral part of all subsequent transactions involving the land and means that if you buy land that has a mortgage registered against it, then you become responsible for repaying the mortgage.

In all property transactions in Portugal, therefore, it is most

important to ensure that not only do you have good title to the
land (ie that you own the land and therefore everything that's
put on it) but also that there are no mortgages or debts
outstanding on the property that you might inherit when you
buy the land. All this information is contained in the local
property register where the property is situated. Making sure
that you do have good title to the property is no work for
the amateur and it is **strongly** recommended that you engage
legal help to do this.

The seller should supply you with a copy of **his** *escritura* which
will show the official address of the property and the
registration number of the property in the property register.
Armed with this information you can now contact the local
property register (by filling in the appropriate forms see Form
B) for information about the property. You can request a search
(a *certidao de teor*) which will provide you simply with the
actual owner of the property or you can take a safer way out
and obtain a certified copy of all the current 'descriptions and
inscriptions'. 'Descriptions' include all matters which are
strictly related to the property such as the area, what it
includes and so on. 'Inscriptions' on the other hand show
the names of the owners, mortgages, mortgage charges,
options, the fact that planning permission has been granted
or *loteamento* has been registered. If the property has still not
yet been registered (for example, because it is a flat in the
course of construction) or was not registered at the time of
the seller's purchase, you will need to go back to the seller
for further information (including the title number to his land
or copy of the receipt of the application to register the
property). You may find on the search certificate the words
'*nao descrito*' meaning 'not described'. This means that the
property has not been registered. Make absolutely sure that
it will be before proceeding any further.

This first simple check should be carried out as early as
possible in the transaction in order that you can avoid major
problems later on.

The promissory contract

In Portugal, a contract drawn up to cover the purchase and sale of any property is known as the promissory contract of purchase and sale. It is known as 'promissory', because both parties effectively promise to enter into the final contract to buy and sell the property (and this is done at a later stage before a notary). Do remember that there are no national Portuguese conditions of sale, or the like, so it is up to you to negotiate the best terms.

Formalities

The contract for the sale and purchase of land is only valid if it is signed by both parties. In addition, if the contract relates to the sale of a house or an apartment (regardless of its state of construction), the signatures of both parties must be witnessed in front of a notary who at the same time will certify (if the property is in course of construction), that a valid building licence has been issued. Failure to adhere to these formalities results in the contract for the purchase and sale of the building being void (but you should note that this provision doesn't apply to the purchase of land).

This provision actually protects you quite well. The seller cannot claim that the contract is invalid because of the lack of formalities, unless he can prove that it was your fault. This particular rule was brought in by the Portuguese Government to protect purchasers against unscrupulous builders and developers selling buildings which did not have planning permission. Because of high inflation, a builder would prefer to renege on the contract and sell the property to someone else at a much higher price (despite having to pay the purchaser twice the amount of the deposit – see later under 'Breach of contract').

It also protects you to a certain extent if you are pressurised

B—Application to local property register

Requisição de CERTIDÃO   Mod. B (art.º 111.º 2 CRP)

Conservatória do Registo Predial de...

Requisitante

Nome e estado ....

Residência:..

B. I. n.º............. de ..../.................../................,de .... Telef. ....

Requisição

N.º.................................... Preparo ....

Data ..../............/........... Rubrica do functionário.........................

Certidão pretendida	N.ºº das descrições/freguesia
☐ Teor da(s) decrição(ões)	
☐ Teor da(s) descrição(ões) e inscrição(ões) a favor do último pro prietário	
☐ Teor da(s) descrição(ões) e de todas as inscrições em vigor	
☐ Teor da(s) descrição(ões) e....................................	
☐ Teor d	
.... arquivado sob o n.º ....,em ...... /...... /......	
☐	
Obs.:...	

O requisitante,

into signing a contract and later decide to change your mind. In law, if the signatures of both parties have not been witnessed in front of a notary, then you are entitled to withdraw from the contract and to reclaim any cash that you have paid. However, the law is one thing – reality is another. If you've paid over a cheque and it's been cashed, it's going to be very difficult to recover it and you may end up having to take legal action against the developer. If you are in the UK and the developer is in Portugal then that is not going to be easy, no matter how strong your legal case. The moral is clear – if you sign any form of contract and pay over any money at all, make absolutely certain that it really is the property you want.

Content of the promissory contract

Parties to the contract

The contract must clearly identify the parties to the contract, stating their names, marital status, address and so on. If you are not sure in whose name you wish the property to be bought (ie in your name, or jointly with your spouse or in the name of an offshore company), then you should make quite sure that the contract states that the purchaser will be you or any other person or organisation that you nominate. By doing this, it will prevent you having to go through the tedious process of either amending the existing contract or even drawing up a new contract if you change your mind later on.

Property

The property must be fully described. It should state not only the address of the property but also refer to the official description of the property in the land registry. It should also include the land registration number. If you have had a search made on the property before you sign the contract (and it is advisable that you should do so), then this will avoid any unpleasant surprises later on ie finding out that you have in fact bought a different apartment or the piece of land next door.

Price

The price of the property should be included in the contract and it can be stated either in *escudos* or in any other foreign currency. The terms of payment should be included and, most important of all, it should make quite clear what the deposit payable on signature will be (and it will not usually exceed 10% of the purchase price). If the deposit is more than 50%, the Bank of Portugal may well query it and you could have problems at a later stage, ie when you apply for your import licence. It's therefore important to insist that if the property is to be paid for in stages that no more than 50% is to be paid before the import licence is issued. Any deposit paid before the import licence is issued will require proof of transfer into Portugal (unless both parties are non-resident). It is important to make sure that the clearing bank is aware when it receives the money that it is money for the deposit (see chapter 8).

Essential covenants

It is absolutely essential that the contract states that the seller will transfer title of the property to you free of all charges and incumbrances and free of any rental agreements.

Completion

The contract should state when completion is to take place. This should not be (as in the UK) by reference to a certain day but should refer instead to the day on which the import licence is granted. You should normally ask that completion takes place within 60 days of that date.

The contract should state in which notarial office the *escritura* is to be signed (preferably the one of your choice or you may find yourself having to travel some distance to the seller's notary) and which of the parties shall notify the other of this signing. It is wise to request that at least 30 days' notice is given that the *escritura* is going to be signed on a certain day.

Breach of contract

Breach of contract by the seller

If, after the promissory contract has been signed, the seller decides he no longer wishes to sell you the property, then you can either force him to sell it to you (known as 'specific performance') or accept compensation equal to twice the amount of any deposit that you have paid. To be realistic, specific performance could well involve your taking legal proceedings against the seller – and that's going to be difficult to achieve in practice. The best solution all round might be to accept everything with good grace and take the money (if you have paid a deposit).

Breach of contract by you

If you have signed a valid promissory contract to purchase a property and then later decide not to go through with the purchase, then your principal loss is your deposit. Once again, the seller could force you to buy the property (ie specific performance) but this is extremely unlikely since neither you nor any of your assets that he could seize as compensation are likely to be in Portugal! If, however, the contract is void for lack of formalities, you are entitled to get your deposit back. However, this would involve court action and might take some time.

Delay in effecting the *escritura*

If you suspect (or if you are told) that the *escritura* is likely to be delayed then providing that the contract has been properly notarised, you may register the contract at the local land registry. This will then give you some protection against the seller selling the property to someone else. However, this form of registration (known as provisional registration of acquisition), does require the consent of the seller and both of you will need to sign the form of provisional registration and your signatures will have to be recognised by the notary. This procedure may be compulsory if you are borrowing

money from a bank to buy your property (see chapter 8).
Provisional registration is valid for six months but may be
renewed at a cost. Alternatively, the promissory contract may
be done by deed, with the result that its subsequent
registration is valid without time limit.

The conveyancing of property

The most common word you will hear in dealing with
property purchases in Portugal is the *escritura*. This means
'deed' and there are all kinds of *escrituras* in the Portuguese
legal system. The one in connection with property purchase
is called the *escritura de compra e venda* which roughly
translates as the deed of purchase and sale, ie the conveyance.

If you are buying a second-hand house or a new house that
has already been built, then the *escritura de compra e venda* will
cover both the land and all the buildings that have been
constructed on that land. If, however, you are buying a plot
of land on which you intend to build or are buying a plot of
land on which there is a house partially constructed, then
the *escritura* will cover the land only.

In England, the signing of the various documents by the
buyer and seller can take place at different places and at
different times, and often in the presence of their own legal
adviser. The exchanging of contracts is often handled by the
respective solicitors with the buyer and seller rarely being in
attendance. In Portugal, on the other hand, the signing is
done in front of a notary, a public official whose job it is to
draw up an agreement that has already been reached between
the buyer and seller.

As a purchaser, you can either sign the *escritura* yourself or
you can give someone else (a lawyer, a member of your
family or a trusted friend) a power of attorney to sign on your
behalf.

Occasionally you may be asked by the promoter or sales organisation to give them or someone in their office a power of attorney to sign the *escritura* on your behalf. You must use your own judgment on this but it's not recommended because a power of attorney may be phrased in **general** terms and this could permit them to buy anything on your behalf which is probably something you wouldn't wish them to do. Powers of attorney are always best given to lawyers who can always be more easily sued for not acting in accordance with your instructions. A specific power of attorney (ie power to buy a particular property) is always safer.

The role of the notary

The role of the notary is to draw up the contract of purchase and sale of the property. It is normal to send drafts to the notary identifying the parties, the property, the price that has been paid for it and any other clauses which are relevant to the use of the property. Before the notary can draw up the *escritura* he will require evidence that everything is legal and above board. In particular he will require the following documents:

1 If you are a tourist, he will need the relevant copy of the import licence (see chapter 8).
2 If the property was built after 1951 he will require evidence of satisfactory completion ie, the certificate of habitation.
3 He will also need proof of the description and inscription numbers in the local land registry, which can be provided by presenting a current certificate of registration or a search (*certidao de teor*) issued within the last three months.
4 He will also need to be shown the *caderneta predial* (showing the current owner of the property). This is a certificate issued by the tax department in the name of the seller confirming that the property has been registered for tax purposes. It must show the taxable value, known as '*valor tributavel*'.

5 A property registered in the tax department is given a matrix number. In the event that the property does not have such a number then the notary will require evidence that an application has been made for registration. This is done by simply providing the notary with a copy of the application which must not be over six months old.

6 The tax department register will also describe the property and it is essential that this description and what it consists of does not conflict with the description at the land registry. If the two do not tie up then the notary will require evidence that an application has been made for rectification.

7 If an attorney is signing the *escritura* on your behalf then he will have to present the notary with the power of attorney. A power of attorney is valid in Portugal if it has been executed at the Portuguese Consulate nearest to you or (if executed before a notary public) bears an *apostille* in accordance with the Hague Convention of 1963. An *apostille* (which can be obtained from the Foreign and Commonwealth Office) is a form stuck on the back of the power of attorney. Although the terms of the convention state that the *apostille* does not require translation many notaries in Portugal refuse to accept the power of attorney unless the *apostille* itself has been officially translated.

8 A receipt from the tax department showing that purchase tax (known as *Sisa* – see chapter 13) has been paid.

9 If the property is being bought by co-ownership, a draft of the co-ownership agreement will be written into the *escritura* or attached to it. If you are buying an apartment, the notary will need to see the certificate of registration of the deed of horizontal property.

An appointment then has to be made with the notary for signing the *escritura*. When you attend the notarial office, the notary will already have entered the contract in his notarial books and will merely read it to you and then invite you to sign. The *escritura* for purchase and sale will be written in Portuguese and if you do not understand Portuguese then you will also need a translator to be present. The translator will be asked to translate the document verbally to you and will then ask you if you have understood the contents of the document and if it is in conformity with your wishes. However, an interpreter is not necessary if the notary himself speaks English and can translate the document to you verbally.

After you have signed the *escritura* you will need to organise certified photocopies with the clerk of the notarial office. It is always wise to order at least two copies: one for use at the land registry and another for your own use. A fee will be charged for each notarised photocopy you require. The notarial fee for effecting the *escritura* will be based not only on the price of the property but also on the number of pages in the *escritura* and also the amount of stamp duty. Roughly speaking the fee will amount to 1% of the purchase price of the property.

Registration

Although the notary will have conferred legal title to the property to you, this will only be valid as between you and the seller. Consequently, at this stage, the ownership of the property is not secure and it won't be until an application has been filed for registration at the local land registry.

The sorts of thing that can still go wrong at this stage are, for example:

- The seller, having cashed your cheque, can take another buyer to another notary's office and make another *escritura*. If the second *escritura* gets to the property registry first then that is the one which will be inscribed in the register.
- The seller might take out a mortgage on the property after he has sold it to you, or his creditors (the tax collector for example) might put an embargo on the property after the *escritura* has been issued.

In such cases, the property registrar might refuse to enter the *escritura* (if another buyer was faster than you in getting his *escritura* to the register) or they may return it to you saying that the *escritura* has no effect on the embargo or mortgage already entered. This is not a feature of life which is peculiar to buying property in Portugal; as in England, previous registrations always take precedence over subsequent registrations.

There are three basic precautions that you can take:

1 Employ a reputable lawyer and choose one that is independent – not necessarily the lawyer suggested to you by the seller.
2 Instruct your lawyer to get an extract from the property register **just before** you sign the *escritura*.
3 Do everything you can to make sure that the *escritura* gets to the property registry as soon as possible after you have signed it. You can do this by collecting the notarised photocopies from the notary as soon as they are ready and taking them to the land registry yourself and applying for registration. You will need to fill in a form for registration which will be marked by the clerks in the land registry so that it takes precedence over any other *escritura* that might be presented.

In due course, you will receive a certificate of registration from the land registry (see Form C) showing that the ownership of the property has now been registered in your name. The certificate will bear the property registry's official stamp which will show the book and the page where the inscription has been made. You must also register at the local tax department obtaining either a new or an updated *caderneta predial*.

You can now relax – the property is yours.

Your title to the property

Now that you have obtained title to your property, what kind of rights have you acquired? As was said at the start of the chapter, there are three types of outright ownership of a property. In addition to being the sole owner, you could share the ownership with other people (co-ownership) or you could buy an apartment under the system of horizontal property. If you choose either of these last two methods, what rights do you have?

Co-ownership

There is of course nothing wrong with clubbing together with family or friends to form a group of people who are interested in buying a property in Portugal for their joint use. There are two ways in which this private 'timesharing' can be done:

1   You can, as a group of individuals, buy a property outright in Portugal with all your individual names listed in the *escritura*. This would normally only be recommended for small groups of people (say no more than four) because the problems of sorting out the legal details with a larger group can be quite difficult.
2   A group of people could get together and form a company in the UK with the company then buying the property in Portugal. This is a simpler route because the legal details are being handled by one entity (ie the company). You will find more details about setting up a company in chapter 5.

In many respects, this is no different from the growing practice of 'joint ownership' in the UK. Faced with the rapidly increasing costs of properties, it is now quite common for two or more people to get together and pool resources in order that they can get a foot on the housing ladder. Once again, there are no legal problems involved in doing this but as

C—Certificate of Registration

CONSERVATÓRIA DO REGISTO PREDIAL
DE

....

———

CERTIDÃO

CERTIFICO que : ————————————————————

a) — as ....fotocópias apensas a esta certidão, de folhas ....a
folhas ...., estão conforme com os originais e foram elas por mim numeradas
e rubricadas, levando aposto o selo branco desta Conservatória;

b) — foi requisitada sob o n.º ....em ....de ....de 198....e
entre a data da respectiva requisição e a sua passagem não foi requisitado outro acto de
registo sobre o(s) prédio(s) adiante mencionado(s) ....

c) — são, respectivamente, o(s) teor(es) da(s) descrição(ões) e da(s) inscrição(ões) de titularidade
e dos encargos em vigor, tudo respeitante a ....
...........................prédio(s) n.º⁽ˢ⁾ ....
....
....

a ~~fls.~~ ....   ~~do(s)~~
Livro(s) B— ....
ou da(s) ficha(s) da(s) freguesia(s) ....
....
....
....
....

CONTA :   ....de ....de 198....

Art.º 11.º, n.º 1 . . . .$00

»   »   n.º 2 . . . .$00

Soma . . . .$00   **O Ajudante,**

Art.º 68.º Dec. 519-F $00

TOTAL $00

(São ....
....
...........................escudos)

Registada sob o n.º ....em ..../ ..../ 19....

Formato A4 — 210x297
53-N — Tip. Nabão, Lda-Tomar

with all co-ownerships it is most important that you agree amongst yourselves exactly what the rules are going to be in the future.

Consequently, if you are considering entering into this kind of arrangement with friends (or even your family) it would be very much in your interests seriously to consider drawing up a legal agreement between the members of the group so as to make it quite clear exactly what their rights and responsibilities are. Like most agreements, it will be designed to resolve problems before they arise – if you can't sort out your problems in advance, then perhaps you should think twice about buying your property with other people!

Amongst the sort of things this agreement should cover (and it can be easily drawn up through a solicitor in the UK) are the following:

- In what proportions are the individuals in the group going to pay for the property? There's no particular need for everybody to contribute an equal share but it should be clearly laid out that when the property is sold, each person receives back the equivalent proportion of the net proceeds.
- What proportion of the running costs is each person going to pay? This could well be done on an equal basis (on the grounds that it's difficult to divide up an electricity bill) but it could equally be done on the basis of usage over a twelve month period.
- What rights of access will each person have to the property? Will it just be by general agreement on a casual basis or will you allocate specific periods of the year to each person on a rota basis?
- When you're entering into this kind of agreement, you will expect it to run for a number of years. However, you should all agree on a certain date in the future when people can withdraw from the scheme and demand their share of the property, in cash. Your agreement should also cover what has to be done in those circumstances, for example:

— Does the property have to be sold?
— Can the other members buy out the share and, if so, on what basis is the price to be agreed?
— Can other people buy into the group and if so, on what basis?

● Emergencies can, and do, arise. What action would be taken if one member is quite unable to continue with the agreement because of financial problems, or death?

Once again, the list is not meant to be exhaustive and you may well have to draw up your own list. The only possible way of approaching this kind of agreement is to try and imagine every possible set of circumstances that could give rise to problems and make sure you have a solution for them.

Co-ownership is becoming increasingly popular and, given the right legal framework for it to operate, there's no reason why it shouldn't be an ideal way of buying property in Portugal.

You do need to pay special attention to the position on death. Under Portuguese law co-ownership exists whenever one or more persons own property rights simultaneously over one given property. In England, co-ownership comes under two different forms: joint tenancy and tenancy in common.

Joint tenants

If you buy a property together with your husband or wife you will usually buy as 'joint tenants'. This means that in the event of either of your deaths the property will pass automatically to the survivor.

Tenants in common

If you purchase a property with another person as tenants in common, then if, you die, your share of the property will be inherited by your legal heirs or beneficiaries as stated under your Will.

In Portugal the concept of joint tenancy does not exist and you will therefore need to write a Will if you intend to leave the property to the person who jointly owns the property with you.

It is within the legal framework of co-ownership that, for example, quarter share schemes (ie where four families club together and buy a property for their joint use) are to be found. The agreement which you will sign regarding the actual use of the property will need to be archived, ie when you sign the *escritura*. It then becomes a **legal** agreement for use of the property and will be interpreted in accordance with Portuguese law.

Selling jointly owned property

If you want to sell your share in the property, you must give notice to the other co-owners, informing them of the price and enclosing a copy of the proposed contract of sale. The other co-owners then have eight days (or whatever longer time limit you have decided on) to inform you whether or not they wish to exercise their right of pre-emption. If more than one co-owner wants to buy your share then it will be divided between them in accordance with the percentage of the property that they already have.

If a co-owner gifts or sells his share in the property **without** giving notice then any of the other co-owners may request the courts to cancel the conveyance and transfer the property to them. Provided they deposit the total value of the price stated in the deed of transfer within eight days of being notified by the court of intended proceedings, the courts will transfer the property to the claiming co-owners.

If you wish to sell your share and you cannot find a purchaser (and your other co-owners don't want to buy your share at the price you are asking) you can apply to the courts for the division of the property. This is a fairly simply procedure; in the absence of any agreement the judge will simply order the property to be auctioned and the proceeds will be divided up between all the co-owners.

It would be quite usual to have a clause in your private agreement (which must be incorporated in the *escritura*) that restricts the selling of the property for a period of, say, four years. This then gives everybody the guarantee that they have a certain period of unrestricted enjoyment to use the property. On the other hand, it also makes sense to have a clause in your agreement which says that after a certain period of time, any of the owners wishing to sell is perfectly entitled to do so regardless of the outcome to the other co-owners. Consequently, you could agree a moment in time (which Portuguese law requires should not be more than five years after the date of the agreement) when all the co-owners then need to seek the agreement of each other regarding the continued use of the property for a further period of no more than five years. If, at that time, one of the co-owners wishes to sell, then the existing co-owners have the right of first refusal to his share of the property.

Buying an apartment

Whereas in England apartments are generally bought leasehold for a term of years, in Portugal the concept of leasehold does not exist. Apartments are therefore sold with absolute title, ie freehold, under the system of 'horizontal property'. This system applies only to apartments which are built as independent units with a separate entrance.

Before you can buy an apartment the builder or developer must effect a deed before the notary constituting the system of horizontal property. The notary will not do this unless the builder shows him all the building plans which must have been approved by the local authority. The whole object of the deed of horizontal property is to create a separate legal title for each individual apartment which will then have to be registered at the local land registry who will give new title numbers for each apartment. The deed of horizontal property and its registration may be effected before the building is completed. In this case registration will be provisional until such time as the building has been approved by the local authority who will issue the appropriate habitation certificate.

If you are thinking of obtaining a mortgage to purchase an apartment, it is absolutely essential that you enquire from the builder whether or not the deed of horizontal property has been duly constituted and registered. If it hasn't then you will have to make him agree that the purchase price will be paid on the date of the signing of the *escritura* conveying the title to you. This is because until such time as the deed of horizontal property has been registered, the apartment does not legally exist and therefore the bank cannot take security for the loan which it would normally do by registering a provisional mortgage against the title of the apartment. Do not forget to make a search against the title of the apartment block to see if the builder has obtained finance from a bank and mortgaged the block to them. If this is the case, you must ask to see some evidence (ie a letter from the bank) that the mortgage will be realised when you complete your purchase.

One of the things that the deed of horizontal property will state is what things constitute the communal parts of the property. Apart from obvious matters such as the ground on which the property is built, the roof, staircases and so on it should also deal with patios, gardens and garages. When purchasing an apartment within a complex which also has a swimming pool, it is absolutely vital to ascertain what rights you or your guests have (and, more importantly, your tenants in the event that you may wish to let the property), to use the pool. The answers will be found in the deed of horizontal property which may or may not include the swimming pool as part of the common areas of the building. The deed may also contain restrictions on the way you use the property and in this respect you will probably find provisions in it which are very similar to those contained in an English lease; the purpose of the two documents, although different in nature, is similar.

The deed will also cover the rules on the administration and maintenance of common parts of the building which under general law is the responsibility of all the owners of the apartments. A meeting of owners must be held at least once a year in January to discuss and approve the accounts of expenditure incurred on the building during the previous year and also to approve the budget for the following year. The position of administrator is salaried and is for a period of two years which can be extended. The functions of the administrator are essentially to ensure that the property is being correctly maintained, to keep the building insured, to keep proper accounts of expenditure, to recover outstanding amounts from the owners and to represent the owners before any local authorities or before the courts.

8 You and the banks

Buying property involves money and that means banks. It is important to get this underway as soon as you are serious about buying your property – and that you understand how the system works.

The basic rules

When you buy property in Portugal, you must pay for it with foreign currency. This establishes your right to take your currency out of Portugal again if you should sell your property. In order to do that, it's necessary for you to prove that you imported foreign currency which has then been exchanged into *escudos* and you do this by means of an import licence – a *boletim de autorizacao de importacao de capitais privados*.

Exchange control in Portugal

All non-resident foreigners are obliged to obtain an import licence for the importation of foreign capital into Portugal if the capital is to be used for buying property. If you don't follow this procedure, there are two implications:

1   The notary will not effect the *escritura* and transfer the title of the property to you unless a copy of the import licence is in the notary's possession to be attached to the *escritura*.

2   When you come to sell your property at a later date, you
    may not be able to repatriate your capital.

When you eventually sell your property then you can apply
for an export licence to allow you to export the proceeds of the
sale outside Portugal but this will only be granted if you
obtained an import licence in the first place. In order to
obtain your export licence, you have to apply to the Bank of
Portugal and this will normally be done by your lawyer or
your bank.

Obtaining your import licence

Before you can obtain your import licence, it's necessary to
be able to prove that you have contracted to buy a property.
The information that has to be supplied to the Bank of
Portugal for an import licence to be granted is as follows:

- The application form – which actually consists of two
  separate forms. One is to deal with the importation of
  currency (see form D); the other deals with the actual
  acquisition of the property and this form has to be signed
  by your lawyer or your bank.
- A letter of authority authorising an application for an
  import licence to be made or a copy of the power of
  attorney which you have given to the person representing
  you in the purchase (unless the application is being made
  via a Portuguese bank).
- A copy of the promissory contract of purchase and sale
  (although this can be replaced by a declaration of sale
  signed by both parties).
- If you are buying land in a development you will need to
  provide a copy of the *loteamento* unless the developer has
  already registered it with the Bank of Portugal.
- If you are buying rustic land then the Bank of Portugal
  will also require a copy of the Opinion from the Ministry
  of Agriculture, in accordance with Decree Law 38/86 (see
  chapter 6).

- If you are buying a timeshare property, you will need to provide:

  — a photocopy of the maintenance contract for the development
  — a photocopy of the certificate that the development has been classified as having 'touristic utility'
  — a photocopy of the promissory contract if available.

- If a deposit has been paid before you obtain your import licence, you will need a *bordereau* from your bank which is confirmation that the money has been received in Portugal and is part of the purchase price.
- If you are borrowing money from abroad to buy the property, you will need to provide a copy of the offer letter (and details of the amount to be borrowed and the rate of interest have to be entered on form D). For loans in Portugal, you need a copy of the offer letter.

For the time being, the application must be submitted (by a person who is a resident of Portugal, usually either your lawyer or bank representative) to the Bank of Portugal who are currently the only organisation who can issue import licences. It is anticipated that new legislation will soon be passed enabling the clearing banks to issue these licences and this should speed up the process. However, in the meantime, you should be warned that an import licence can take at least three months to be issued.

The licence will be issued in respect of foreign currency imported into Portugal. It will not be issued in respect of any Portuguese *escudos* that you bring into the country or that you have there already.

Importing currency

Transferring sterling from the UK to Portugal is not difficult. You can either do this from your existing UK bank or from a Portuguese bank with a branch in London. You will have

D—Application for import licence

BANCO DE PORTUGAL	BOLETIM DE AUTORIZAÇÃO DE IMPORTAÇÃO DE CAPITAIS PRIVADOS	REF. EØE ___	BAICP N.º	A

REQUERENTE

NOME ___

DOMICILIO ___

LOCALIDADE ___

PAÍS ___

REMETENTE

NOME ___

DOMICÍLIO ___

LOCALIDADE ___

PAÍS ___

REPRESENTADO POR

NOME ___

DOMICILIO ___

LOCALIDADE ___

OPERAÇÃO

CURTO PRAZO [1]
M/L PRAZO [2]

MOEDA CONTRATUAL ___

MOEDA(S) LIQUIDAÇÃO ___

MONTANTE CONTRATUAL

DESCRIÇÃO DA OPERAÇÃO

N.º _____ da classe _____.ª do Anexo ao Decreto-Lei n.º 183/70, de 28 de Abril

CRÉDITO EXTERNO   **BANCOS AVALISTAS**

COM AVAL DO ESTADO [1] ___ %

COM GARANTIA BANCÁRIA [2] ___ %

SEM GARANTIA BANCÁRIA [3] ___ %

TAXA DE JURO { FIXA [1]   VARIÁVEL [2] }   BASE ___   SPREAD ___

RELACIONADO COM O BAECP N.º ___

PRAZO CONTRATUAL ___

PROJECTO   ANOS   MESES

| R | D | Ø | | CÓDIGO ESTATÍSTICO | | DATA DO CONTRATO |

CONDIÇÕES VINCULATIVAS ESPECIAIS

SIM [1]   NÃO [2]

BANCO DE PORTUGAL

DATA DE EMISSÃO   DATA DE VALIDADE

AUTORIZADO NOS TERMOS DO DEC.-LEI N.º 183/70, DE 28 DE ABRIL.

Mod. 32057-2 - A4 - 40.000 ex. - 10/86

to bear the costs of conversion and you can also expect to pay a handling charge if sending money by telex (although if you are borrowing funds from your bank for property purchase, these charges will usually be waived).

It is essential that the foreign currency you import into Portugal is credited by the Portuguese clearing bank to the import licence (and they are obliged to notify the Bank of Portugal that the money has been received). If, and when, you eventually apply for an export licence, you will have to account for any discrepancy between the amount applied for in the licence and the amount imported.

An import licence is valid for 90 days (although the Bank of Portugal often now issue them for 180 days) and during this timescale you should ensure that all the formalities of buying your property are completed. If you hit any particular difficulties, you can apply to the Bank of Portugal for the licence to be extended for a further 90 or 180 days if required.

Points to bear in mind

One particular point that you should bear in mind is that your import licence is very much tied to the property that you propose to buy. It is, therefore, quite important that you are absolutely sure that the property you currently intend to buy really is the property you want. If you change your mind in the meantime, (ie you might suddenly decide you want to buy another house in a different part of Portugal), then you will have to apply for a new import licence and cancel the previous one. Like all bureaucracies, if you suddenly change your mind in the middle of any process, you will have to start again which will mean considerable delays as you will end up at the back of the queue.

It's also important that you know in whose name the property is going to be bought. If you apply for an import licence in your own name and then later on decide that you want to

own the property jointly with your spouse, then you have
to make an application for rectification (see Form E) of the
original import licence and that will also take time. Another
example might be where you suddenly discover that it would
be more appropriate to put the property in the name of an
offshore company (see chapter 5). In this situation, a
completely *new* import licence application will have to be
made.

One thing that is important is that if you pay any money to
the builder or developer before your import licence is approved,
then the money you transfer to Portugal is noted by the
receiving bank as a payment on account under the terms of
the building contract. You may use funds you have deposited
in a non-resident *escudo* account; such deposits are known
as 'invisibles'. These do **not** get applied to an import licence
but provided the money is used to pay the deposit on a
property and provided the deposit doesn't exceed 50% of the
purchase price then the Bank of Portugal will generally raise
no objections. This is because they are aware of the
commercial realities which is simply that no seller will sign
a promissory contract (see chapter 7) unless he receives a
deposit. However, the new import licence application forms
require documentary evidence (a *bordereau*) that any deposit
paid has been correctly transferred to Portugal.

A major change is that the new licences provide for the
possibility of the purchase money being raised by means of a
loan granted either within or outside Portugal. However, a
distinction will be made between loans granted in Portugal
but having the right of subsequent transfer abroad and those
which do not have such right, reflecting the new mortgage
schemes for the purchase of property where the loan, although
granted in the UK, is actually being financed in Portugal.

E—Application for rectification

BANCO DE PORTUGAL   [A]

BOLETIM DE $\frac{\text{RECTIFICAÇÃO}}{\text{PRORROGAÇÃO}}$ N.° ....

Boletim de autorização de $\frac{\text{Importação}}{\text{Exportação}}$ .de capitais privados n.° .... emitido
em ..../......./........
Requerente (nome, firma ou denominação) ....

....

Residência ou domicílio ....

....

RECTIFICAÇÃO

De: ....

....

....

....

....

Para: ....

....

....

....

....

....

PRORROGAÇÃO

Prazo de validade até .... para efeito de actos notariais
e de registo.

Prazo de validade até .... relativamente à importância
de .... ainda não utilizada.

Autorizado nos termos do Decreto-Lei n.° 183/70, de 28 de Abril.

Lisboa, ...

BANCO DE PORTUGAL
Por delegação

....

Exporting currency

When you eventually sell your property, you will need to apply for an export licence (see Form F) to allow you to take the proceeds of the sale outside Portugal. This will only be granted if you obtained an import licence in the first place. In order to obtain your export licence you have to apply to the Bank of Portugal and this will normally be done by your lawyer or your bank.

If you sell your property to somebody resident outside Portugal then a simultaneous application can be made for an import licence (on behalf of the buyer) and an export licence (on your behalf). This means that the actual proceeds of the sale can be paid outside Portugal once the import licence has been approved and only the money your purchaser will require for the payment of *Sisa*, notarial, registration, legal fees and any other expenses need actually be paid into Portugal.

If you sell to a Portuguese national or to a foreign resident in Portugal who does not hold a current import licence or to a foreign resident who does not wish to export funds, then you will simply apply for an export licence on your own behalf.

To obtain an export licence you will have to apply to the Bank of Portugal and they will need to see a copy of your *escritura* with your original import licence attached to it. The Bank will check that the amount of money that you applied to bring into the country when you purchased your property actually ties up with the amount of money that was credited under the import licence (and if it does not, they will ask for further information which will delay the issuing of your export licence). After the *escritura* has been made for the sale, a copy is then sent to the Bank of Portugal. They will then send a copy of the approved export licence to your clearing bank who will then arrange for the sale proceeds to be transferred back to the UK. New export licence application forms are also being introduced along with those for import licences.

F—Application for Export Licence

BANCO DE PORTUGAL	BOLETIM DE AUTORIZAÇÃO DE EXPORTAÇÃO DE CAPITAIS PRIVADOS	REF. EØE ___	BAECP N.º	A

REQUERENTE
NOME
DOMICILIO
LOCALIDADE
PAÍS

DESTINATÁRIO
NOME
DOMICÍLIO
LOCALIDADE
PAÍS

REPRESENTADO POR
NOME
DOMICILIO
LOCALIDADE

OPERAÇÃO   CURTO PRAZO [1]   M/L PRAZO [2]
MOEDA CONTRATUAL
MOEDA(S) LIQUIDAÇÃO
MONTANTE CONTRATUAL

DESCRIÇÃO DA OPERAÇÃO   N.º ___ da classe ___.ª do Anexo ao Decreto-Lei n.º 183/70, de 28 de Abril

CRÉDITO EXTERNO   **BANCOS AVALISTAS**
COM AVAL DO ESTADO [1]   %
COM GARANTIA BANCÁRIA [2]   %
SEM GARANTIA BANCÁRIA [3]   %
TAXA DE JURO { FIXA [1] VARIÁVEL [2] }   BASE ____   RELACIONADO COM O BAICP N.º ____
SPREAD ____   PRAZO CONTRATUAL ____   ANOS MESES
PROJECTO
R | D | Ø | CÓDIGO ESTATÍSTICO ____   DATA DO CONTRATO ____

CONDIÇÕES VINCULATIVAS ESPECIAIS   SIM [1]   NÃO [2]

BANCO DE PORTUGAL   DATA DE EMISSÃO ____   DATA DE VALIDADE ____

AUTORIZADO NOS TERMOS DO DEC.-LEI N.º 183/70, DE 28 DE ABRIL.

Mod. 02058:2 – A4 – 30 000 ex. – 4/87

On 1 January 1989, capital gains tax was extended (see chapter 13). The impact is that you will be able to export currency resulting from the sale of your property only after payment of capital gains tax. This only applies in the case of properties which were purchased after 1 January 1989.

Invisibles

Very often, when you buy land with the intention of building on it, two import licences will have been granted to you; one for the purchase of the land and the other to cover the amounts due under the building contract. However, because a notary only requires a valid import licence in respect of the land to convey this to you, there is a temptation on the part of both builders and agents to import the money correctly under the import licence in connection with the **land** but not for the **building**. This will result in these monies being imported as 'invisibles' and not under a valid import licence. In these circumstances, the Bank of Portugal will want to know how the cash for the building was brought into Portugal (since you will be selling both the land and the property) and may pose all sorts of problems. They may, in the end, refuse to issue an export licence for the total sale price. The moral is to make quite sure that **all** the money you need in connection with the purchase of your property is credited to an import licence.

If you sell your property to a Portuguese national or an EEC resident national who does not hold an import licence, the capital can be exported provided the cash was originally imported correctly to Portugal. At the present time, the Portuguese legislation allows for up to 160,000 ECUs (European Currency Units) but this limit is due to be increased each year until 1992, when exchange control allegedly ceases in Portugal for EEC residents. It should be noted, however, that Portugal has successfully applied to the EEC for permission that the exchange control regulations should continue until 1995.

Banking in Portugal

Banking for tourists

The first thing to take note of is that there's a further complication in Portuguese law regarding the definition of residence for banking purposes, ie over and above your resident status for immigration and tax purposes. In Portugal, you are only considered as a resident for **banking purposes** when a year has elapsed after you have been granted residence by the Service of Foreign Nationals (see chapter 15).

There are three types of bank account that a tourist can open:

1   A tourist account in *escudos*.
2   A non-resident *escudo* account.
3   Sterling and other foreign currency accounts.

Tourist escudo account

A tourist *escudo* account is just like a current account in the UK. It is an account that you will use for day-to-day expenses and it is this account on which you will draw all cheques, and arrange standing orders.

You will be able to transfer cash to this account from abroad providing it is made through your bank. If you use your account to purchase small amounts of foreign currency, then you can recredit any unused amounts of foreign currency when you come back into Portugal.

You can use your account for paying all your holiday expenses, and all your tax payments, rates, maintenance costs and other service costs incurred while using your property. Apart from that, no interest is paid on this account and it is not allowed to go overdrawn.

Non-resident escudo account

The main purpose of this type of account is to fulfil the
residence permit requirements of people wishing to move to
Portugal for the purposes of taking up employment in a
service industry (see chapter 15). However, the Bank of
Portugal may also authorise the opening of a non-resident
escudo account for the purpose of purchasing property in
Portugal. You will need to write to your Portuguese bank
(quoting your full name and UK address with a photocopy
of your passport), stating clearly that the funds which will be
deposited in the account will eventually be used for the
purchase of property. Credits to this account must be made
in foreign currency and funds deposited may be used for
paying the deposit on a property (ie you can set your property
purchase process in motion without having to wait for an
import licence). Nevertheless, this doesn't mean that you need
not obtain an import licence – you will not be able to
complete the legal process on buying your property without
an import licence covering the full declared value in the
escritura.

Sterling and other foreign currency accounts

These are very straightforward and can be opened by any
non-resident. You can have cheques paid into it direct from
your bank in the UK or from any other bank account you
hold in any other part of Europe. You can also buy foreign
currency from your bank in the UK and transfer it to your
foreign currency accounts in Portugal.

In order to open one of these accounts, you will have to make
a fairly high initial deposit (approximately £2,500) and you'll
be required to leave it in that account for at least 30 days.
You will also need to provide your bank in Portugal with
proof of residence abroad – this would normally be a letter
from your UK bank.

Chequebooks are not issued for foreign currency accounts but
they do earn interest (and interest rates are of course variable
from time to time). Tax at 20% is withheld from all interest

payments and you are then given a certificate of tax
deduction in order to complete your tax return.

Banking for residents

Once you are resident for banking purposes in Portugal (ie at
least 12 months after you have been granted residence by
the Service of Foreign Nationals), you will have to close the
accounts you opened as a tourist and open your resident's
accounts instead. You are allowed to hold current or deposit
accounts in *escudos* and these have exactly the same kind of
use as current and deposit accounts in the UK. The interest
rates earned on deposits vary from time to time and tax at
20% is deducted from the interest at source although you will
also get a certificate of tax deduction in order to help you
complete your tax return.

The movement of currency

Since Portugal joined the European Community, the rules on
the movement of currency have been eased slightly. If you
are a resident, it is possible for you to take into Portugal
50,000 *escudos* in notes or coins or foreign currency up to
the equivalent of 150,000 *escudos*.

If you are a non-resident, then you can bring an unlimited
amount of foreign currency into the country (including
travellers cheques) but only up to 50,000 *escudos* in notes or
coins.

When you leave Portugal, you can take out the same amount
of *escudos* but you need special authorisation if the amount
exceeds 100,000 *escudos* in value. If the amount exceeds the
equivalent of 50,000 *escudos* then you will have to provide
proof that you had more than that amount on you when you
came into Portugal or that you've received the cash whilst
in Portugal. Cash advances can be received in Portugal either
by direct transfer from your bank in the UK or by cash

advance made against your credit card (although these must be exclusively in *escudos*).

Borrowing money to pay for your property

There are basically several ways in which you can buy your property abroad:

- You can raise the cash from your own personal resources to pay for the property.
- You can raise a mortgage in this country against suitable security (eg your home in the UK) and use the proceeds to buy your property abroad. You should of course note that if you do raise a loan to buy property abroad, then the interest payments do not qualify for tax relief as they would if you were buying your home in this country (on loans of up to £30,000).
- You can raise a mortgage in this country against the security of your property in Portugal. A number of financial institutions in the UK may be willing to lend money against the security of foreign property although you **may** find that your bank will require a guarantee from a foreign bank (the guarantee can be secured on the overseas property but be prepared for a fee of about 1% a year for the guarantee).
- You can raise a loan with a Portuguese bank against the security of your property in Portugal and pay interest to them as you would to a bank in the UK.

UK loans against UK assets

With the rapid increase in house prices this decade, people who have owned a home here for more than a year or two may well have a considerable amount of equity in their property. This equity can be released by means of a re-mortgage or through a further advance and the proceeds used for the purchase of a second home abroad. In general, a mortgage on UK property will offer a wider choice of options than a mortgage using the foreign property as security.

The key advantages of raising a loan against UK property are as follows:

- It allows you to pay for your Portuguese property in cash which could make things very much simpler should you at any time in the future decide to sell your Portuguese property and repatriate the proceeds.
- UK mortgages are commonly granted for longer terms than may generally be obtained from foreign banks. For non-residents, a maximum term of 15 years is common in many European countries – in the UK, terms of 25 years are commonplace and even terms in excess of 30 years are possible.
- The loan is granted and repayable in sterling so there is no exchange rate risk (which could arise if the loan was granted and payable in foreign currency).
- There are no withholding tax problems for UK residents (see later section).
- UK interest rates are often lower than those obtainable from banks in the most popular areas for homes abroad including Portugal.
- UK lending institutions offer a rather more flexible approach to repayment methods than many European banks who will often consider only a straight repayment mortgage.

If you decide to use your existing UK home as the security for a further loan, then you will have to decide whether or not to re-mortgage your property or apply for a further advance. Your first call should be to your current lender (if you are buying your UK home on a mortgage) but it may be necessary to apply to another lender if you need a further advance. In most cases, lenders obviously require adequate security and will normally prefer a first charge on your UK property. However, an increasing number of lenders are prepared to accept a second charge behind another lender although this will usually mean a higher rate of interest.

One important thing to bear in mind when applying for a re-mortgage is the question of tax relief. The rules for mortgage tax relief were modified in the 1988 Finance Act to exclude relief for home improvement loans. If you have an existing loan with a home improvement element on it on which you are obtaining tax relief, the relief on the home improvement element will be lost if the loan is varied, for example by a re-mortgage. Consequently, before deciding to re-mortgage your UK property in order to raise capital to buy a property abroad, you should make quite sure that the tax relief on your existing loan will not be affected in any way.

Even if your existing tax relief is unaffected by the change, adding a non-qualifying loan (and a loan to buy property abroad **is** a non-qualifying loan ie it does not qualify for tax relief on the interest) to your existing mortgage will take the whole loan out of the MIRAS system. This is a factor to be borne in mind if you are self-employed because you will only be able to claim the tax relief on the qualifying part of your mortgage through your tax return.

Another change in the 1988 Finance Act was the restriction of mortgage relief to £30,000 per property, thus ruling out 'double MIRAS' for unmarried couples. The restriction applies to loans effected after 1 August 1988 but existing arrangements are unaffected. It is likely to make good sense, therefore, not to disturb an arrangement that attracts this valuable benefit.

A further advance means asking your existing lender for more funds and while most lenders will be willing to consider this, they may charge you an increased rate of interest for the further advance. In favour of a further advance, there is the fact that you have a pre-existing relationship with your current lender and this should stand you in good stead when applying for the extra money. A re-mortgage could well mean transferring your mortgage to a new lender which will inevitably mean extra costs for legal and valuation fees.

It may, of course, be perfectly acceptable to raise a UK loan against other security and many banks will consider taking a wide range of investment holdings as loan security (eg shares, unit trusts, insurance bonds and so on). The principal disadvantage of this type of loan is that it's likely to be more difficult to arrange than a loan secured against property and its availability will be more dependent on the current financial climate. Also, the maximum loan is unlikely to exceed 60% of the value of the collateral (although it may be more for Government bonds and cash deposits). Also, you may well find that the loan is limited to a period of five years.

Qualifying property

The attitude of the lender may vary according to the type of property you intend to purchase. However, provided you meet their lending criteria you should have no problem raising funds regardless of whether you wish to buy land, a building in progress or a completed property. If you are buying a property which is in course of construction, then the money will usually be advanced in stages in accordance with the progress of construction.

Money lent against a development gives you some reassurance because the lender will be aware of a particular developer's reputation and will only lend money where they know the developer to be sound. However, that is only reassurance – it is not a guarantee. It is still up to you to check that the developer who is arranging the construction of your property is able to do the job he claims to do and is financially stable.

Obtaining a mortgage

If you are thinking of buying a property in Portugal and you need a loan then, before you make an offer on the property, you should first go and talk to your lender to see how much they would be prepared to lend you on your current income (if you are self employed, they will need to see copies of the last three years' accounts). If you have any doubts as to your income qualifications then it would be best to write to them stating what your circumstances are and asking them if, on your financial resources alone, they will be prepared to give you an advance. The sort of things that they would look at are not only the length of your employment but also what other assets you have in the UK and whether these are already subject to an existing mortgage. They will want to make sure that you have sufficient income to service the loan.

In any event, the lender will ask you to complete an application form and after making enquiries regarding your financial status will also obtain a valuation of the property you propose to purchase. The timing of your mortgage offer will vary from lender to lender but you can usually expect an offer in principle within a few days (provided you have supplied all the necessary details about yourself in the application form). The formal offer itself will only be forthcoming when more detailed checks have been done in relation to the property ie when the lender has been reassured that the property is what you claim it to be. Until the mortgage is formally granted, it is important not to enter into any agreements which are legally binding.

Never sign a promissory contract for the property against which you intend to obtain a mortgage unless it contains a clause stating that if a mortgage is not granted then the contract is null and void and any deposit paid on the contract will be immediately refunded.

An import licence application will differ slightly if there is a mortgage involved. The main difference is that the fact that you are obtaining a loan must be noted on the import licence (and the Bank of Portugal will want to see a copy of the loan agreement).

If you obtain a loan half way through your purchase (eg once you have purchased the land and merely require a loan to help you with the cost of building) then the application for the import licence may take somewhat longer to process. This is because there will already have been one (or two) import licences issued in your name (one for the land and one for the building contract) and some money will have already been imported into Portugal under them. Therefore, in order to record the lender's interest on the import licences, rectification of the same will have to be made.

Borrowing from a Portuguese bank

One way you can finance a home in Portugal is by obtaining a loan (which will be secured by a mortgage on your Portuguese property) from one of the Portuguese banks in London. There are currently three banks offering mortgages:

1   Banco Espirito Santo e Commercial de Lisboa at 4, Fenchurch Street, London EC3.
2   Banco Totta & Acores at 68, Cannon Street, London EC4.
3   Banco Portugues do Atlantico at 77, Gracechurch Street, London EC3.

Any person who is resident outside Portugal and whose income is derived from outside Portugal may apply to obtain a loan. If you are already resident in Portugal (or intend to take up permanent residence) you may still apply for a loan **provided** you retain a source of income outside Portugal. If you are approaching retirement (or if you are retired), you may find that your age is a factor as (in common with many UK lenders) the banks will require that the loan is repaid by the time you reach a certain age.

The loan contracts issued by the Portuguese banks tend to be standard English contracts (as used by building societies and other English banks) and are governed under English Law. The security of the loan itself will be governed under

Portuguese law, which states that no mortgage on property is valid unless it is done by an *escritura*.

The Portuguese formalities

Apart from obtaining the necessary import licences, provisional registration of the mortgage will have to be effected as soon as possible at the local land registry. This can be done as soon as the promissory contract has been signed. The appropriate form (see Form G) must be filled in both by you and the seller and both your signatures must be recognised by a notary. At this point, registration fees must be paid. Registration fees are based not only on the price of the property but in this case also on the amount of the loan. You will therefore need to budget for these fees and when you are talking to your bank you should ask them exactly how much these will cost you.

Once the registrar has processed your application he will enter on the registry your provisional acquisition of the property and a provisional mortgage in favour of your bank. This provisional registration (which is valid for six months) means that the property cannot now be sold to anybody else, ie the bank now has security for the loan.

This is why a provisional registration of the mortgage is done before the actual *escritura*. There may be a delay in effecting registration **after** the *escritura* has been effected (some land registries take quite a long time to actually carry out registrations) and therefore the bank will insist on provisional registration to ensure that their own investment is secure.

As soon as this is done, the date for the *escritura* must be fixed. The *escritura* will either transfer the property to you and create a mortgage (or create the mortgage itself if you already own the property). Once the legalised photocopy of the *escritura* is obtained, it must be taken to the land registry who will then convert the provisional registration of acquisition and mortgage (or just mortgage as the case may

G—Application for provisional registration

Requisição de REGISTO   Mod. B (art.º 41.º CRP)

Conservatória do Registo Predial de ....

Apresentante

1 — (a) Coluna reservada aos serviços.

Nome e estado ....

(b) Indicação do n.º de ordem dos actos pedidos.

Residência ....

B. I. n.º ...., de ..../......./......., de .... Telef. ....

(c) Indicação do n.º de ordem dos prédios.

Apresentações	Preparo	Rubrica do funcionário
N.ºˢ	Inicial . . . .$.......	....
Data ......'......./......	Complementar ....../.../..... ....$.......	
	Total . . . .$.......	

2 — Os actos e os documentos juntos devem ser assinalados com uma cruz na quadrícula respectiva.

3 — Registo de aquisição provisória, antes de lavrado o contrato — não sendo junto o contrato promessa, a requisição deve ser assinada pelo(s) titular(es) do(s) prédio(s) a transmitir, com reconhecimento presencial do(s) assinatura(s).

4 — Registo de hipoteca provisória, antes de lavrado o contrato — a requisição deve ser assinada pelo(s) titular(es) do(s) prédio(s) a hipotecar, com reconhecimento presencial do(s) assinatura(s).

5 — Nos casos acima indicados deve ser mencionado o nome completo do adquirente, ou do credor, estado civil e residência ou sede.

Quando casado, deve indicar-se o nome do cônjuge e o regime de bens.

6 — No verso deste impresso devem ser mencionados os elementos necessários ao registo, tais como a causa e o valor da aquisição (i. g. compra ajustada por x), ou o fundamento e o valor da hipoteca (i. g. empréstimo de x ,ao juro anual de ... % e y para despesas).

REQ. ....

REG. ....

(a)	(b)	Actos de registo/Documentos	(c)	Prédios
		☐ Aquisição provisória por natureza a favor de	....	
		....	....	
		....	....	
		....	....	
		....	....	
		....	....	
		....	....	
		☐ Hipoteca provisória por natureza a favor de	....	
		....	....	
		....	....	
		....	....	
		....	....	
		....	....	
		☐ Caderneta predial, conferida em ..../......./.......		
		pela .... Repartição de Finanças de	....	
		☐ Certidão de teor matricial, passada em ....../......./......		
		pela .... Repartição de Finanças de	....	
		☐ Duplicado de participação para inscrição matricial, apresentada em ..../......./......; na .... Repartição de Finanças de	....	
		☐	....	
		....	....	
		....	....	
		☐	....	
		....	....	
		....	....	

(Mod. exclusivo do Cofre C. N. e F. Justiça)   PREÇO: 50$00 be) into a definitive registration. On this occasion a further small fee is payable.

The tax position

There are three main areas where it is important to understand the tax implications before proceeding with the purchase of your property.

Tax relief on the mortgage

Mortgage interest relief is granted against the interest paid on the first £30,000 of a 'qualifying loan' – either by deduction at source (the MIRAS system) or by adjustment to your personal tax code (and, for higher rate taxpayers, a combination of both methods).

A 'qualifying loan' is, for our purposes, a loan granted for the purchase of property in the United Kingdom which is your only or main residence.

Raising a loan to buy property abroad falls outside this definition and therefore UK tax relief is **not** available on the loan interest.

Tax relief against letting income

If you intend to let your property, the income that you receive will be liable to taxation both in the UK and also in Portugal (although there may be relief available under the appropriate double taxation treaty). In the UK, if you own property which is available for letting as holiday accommodation you are allowed to offset the interest that you pay on the loan against the income that you receive from letting. This only applies to UK property – it does **not** apply to foreign property.

Withholding tax

If you enter into any kind of loan agreement with a Portuguese or other overseas bank, make absolutely certain that the loan agreement states that the interest rate that you pay is **after deduction of UK withholding taxes** (this does not apply if the loan is made through a Portuguese bank resident in London to whom the repayments are also made). The reason for this is that if you pay annual interest to any individual or organisation, it is income in their hands and the Inland Revenue may require you to deduct tax at the basic rate from the interest payments. This ensures that the Inland Revenue get their share of the income that you are paying to the person from whom you have borrowed the money. The Revenue may want more money from the lender but they will sort that out themselves.

This principle still applies even if you pay interest abroad. In these circumstances, the tax that you have to deduct and pay to the Revenue is also called withholding tax (although under a double taxation agreement the amount of tax that you are required to deduct from the interest payment will normally be less than the standard rate of withholding tax). Nevertheless, if you have not made sure that your loan agreement states that the interest rate is after deduction of withholding taxes, you could find yourself paying the gross interest to the Portuguese Overseas Bank and the withholding tax to the Inland Revenue.

The moral of this is – if you are looking for a loan from an overseas bank, make sure that you show the agreement to an accountant or solicitor who is familiar with withholding taxes to make sure that you end up paying only the agreed rate of interest and no more.

Repayment methods

There are three principal methods of repaying a mortgage in
the UK:

- The 'repayment' method where you make regular payments
  covering both interest and repayment of capital over the
  term of the mortgage.
- The 'endowment' method where you pay interest only
  throughout the term of the mortgage and repay the loan
  out of the proceeds of a suitable endowment life assurance
  policy.
- The 'pension related' method where you pay interest only
  throughout the term of the mortgage and repay the loan
  when you retire out of the lump sum that you may be
  eligible for under the terms of your pension plan.

Each of these methods has its advantages and disadvantages
and you should discuss the method that is most appropriate
to you with your usual financial adviser.

If you are borrowing money in the UK on the security of
your UK property, you may well have considerable choice of
mortgage repayment method. Borrowing against other
security or borrowing from an overseas bank could mean
that you are obliged to use the repayment terms dictated by
the lender.

9 Things to bear in mind

Whether you are buying a second-hand property, a new house or having a house built, there are a number of points you have to bear in mind. Often, these would not occur to you at home. Here, for example, used to water on tap, it would never occur to us ask if it is salty or not. So this chapter is to alert you to some of the things that you might not have taken into account at the start of your house buying search.

The services

Regardless of the type of property that you are buying, there are certain areas that you need to watch carefully, some of them rather different from those you are used to when buying property in the UK.

Paying for services

In some cases, you may have to pay for the connection of services. Electricity meters, for example, must be installed in your name by the local electricity company. If you are having to get a new connection made from the local supply, together with meter installation, you might find you are paying quite a sizeable sum of money. If you plan to have a phone, check carefully with the telephone company on the costs of installation. If you are in a particularly isolated area, it could cost thousands of pounds. Check before you commit yourself. Check out the position with water. In some areas, the water distribution is the responsibility of a private company and you might find you are having to pay quite a lot of money for connection to the supply.

Water

Although Portugal has a fairly substantial rainfall in total, it doesn't fall evenly over Portugal and the rain that does fall is not particularly well harnessed. Consequently, there is surplus rainfall in the north and a scarcity in the south. Moreover, the rain tends to come in short periods in the south (towards the end of autumn) and, in addition, the south now has to share its water with some six million tourists who come to visit Portugal in the driest part of the year.

Because of this, it's advisable to look into the water situation in the area where you intend to buy. Not surprisingly, the people selling property aren't too keen to talk about it so make a point of asking your prospective new neighbours what the problems are. Above all, be prepared to pay for your water – most houses have a water meter installed by the water authorities and you will pay for it in much the same way as you pay for electricity. This means a standing charge plus a variable charge depending on the amount of water that you use. It's a nuisance but it is by far the safest way of ensuring that you pay the correct amount for your water.

Sweet or sour? In some areas near the coast, you may find that water is being drawn from a very low water table which means that at peak times in the year, the water turns salty. Also, during the peak months, don't be surprised if the water supply is turned off altogether. Under those circumstances, you are going to have to rely on bottled water from the local supermarket or go to the expense of building a *cisterna* which is a sort of large water storage tank. You will need planning permission in order build one of these but, before you do, make sure there is a local supply that is readily accessible to you. Water lorries are not a familiar sight in Britain – they are in Portugal. You might consider a bore

hole on your land from which to fill your *cisterna*, but you
will require permission from your local authority.

You may also find that the water in some areas of Portugal is
very hard and it may be worth your while thinking about
installing a water softener to save any problems in the future
with clogged pipes.

Electricity

In a correctly built urbanisation, the electricity supply will be
to the edge of your plot. In the price of the construction for
the house you should ensure that the electricity connection is
included. You should only have to pay for the contract with
the electricity company and for the meter. If you have chosen
to build your own house, the cost of linking it up to the
mains supply can prove to be as high as a few thousand
pounds, depending on how far you are from the nearest
available supply.

The simplest way to pay for your electricity is through your
bank, via standing order (and you will find details on how
to set this up in chapter 8). The electricity board will take
the money from your bank account and will then send you
a copy of the meter reading showing you how the bill is
calculated.

The telephone

There is one aspect to life in Portugal which you have to get
used to very early on and that concerns the telephone system.
Throughout Portugal, the use of public telephone boxes is
very widespread and they are very easy to use and very
efficient. When it comes to having a phone installed in your
own home, things are very different.

The telephone company in Portugal is a public company
under the supervision of the Government. In each province

the company has a delegation and they are the people to contact when you wish to install a phone. All you have to do is to phone the appropriate number, state that you wish to have a phone installed and they will take a note of your name and address. They will then write to you telling you whether you can have a phone or not and, if you can, the price and the contract conditions. You sign the contract if you agree to pay the price they are quoting and return it to the company. You then sit back and wait for the installation men to come. And wait.

Occasionally, you can be lucky and get a phone installed quickly. In other areas, all the lines are taken and you will wait months if not years for a telephone to be installed. The only sure way to get a phone quickly is to demonstrate to the authorities that you have a real need, either through illness or for the requirements of your business.

The sewerage

Although it's a slightly indelicate subject, do make sure you enquire about the sewage disposal arrangements. Mains sewerage is common on some of the newer developments in the coastal regions but in most other cases you will find that your property is connected to a cesspool (a *fossa*) without any particular problems. Do find out what the arrangements are for the emptying of the cesspit because in some cases you might find that there is a special tax levied by the local municipality to cover this particular problem.

What is important is that you find out where the cesspit covers are because they often require emptying so infrequently that they get covered over, and, most unfortunate of all, occasionally built over by such things as paths or terraces. It's a simple thing to overlook.

Running costs and maintenance

One thing you shouldn't ignore when buying property in Portugal is the running costs. These can mount up to quite significant amounts and it's something you can take account of in advance:

- There will be standing charges on electricity, telephone and water whether you use the services or not.
- Local property rates also have to be taken into account.
- If you live in an urbanisation with community fees, or in an apartment block, then you will have annual charges to pay.
- If you have your own plot with a swimming pool and garden, then you will have monthly maintenance charges to pay for both.
- You will have insurance premiums to pay on the property and contents.

The costs of maintenance

Over and above the running costs, you have to consider the maintenance costs of the property itself. Don't believe that just because you have a home in the sun, it won't require maintenance. The rain in Portugal may fall infrequently but, when it does, it can be almost tropical. Those white houses look lovely in the sunshine – but they soon get dirty and start to look shabby. They're going to need re-painting about once every three years.

Those grilles and railings may look absolutely magnificent when they're first painted, but the influence of the Portuguese sun and possibly a sea breeze or two will soon have that black paint looking less than sparkling. You are going to have to keep your property in good repair and that's something that you may not have thought about. If your property is being used principally for holidays, you don't necessarily want to spend half your holidays with the paintbrush in your hand and although Portugal may have been cheap in the past, you could well find that painters and decorators, particularly in the more popular areas of the Algarve, are just as expensive as in the UK.

Insuring your property

Like all property, you must insure your home and the contents as well. It's occasionally difficult to get an insurance company in this country to insure your property abroad especially if it's being used primarily for holidays. You might find that your own insurance company is more sympathetic but their reluctance is because holiday homes are often left unoccupied for large parts of the year leading to more claims for damage and theft.

You will generally find it slightly more expensive to insure a holiday home abroad and you might find that some of the cover is restricted (for example theft or burst pipes) if the house is left unoccupied for extended periods of time. With some contents cover, you might even find that theft (one of the biggest risks) is excluded entirely so read the small print carefully.

The location of your property will also affect how the policy is taken out. Most of the larger British insurance companies will have offices or agencies in most western European countries. Insurance, therefore, can be arranged in Britain, but it must in order to comply with Portuguese law be issued through the company's office in Portugal.

If your property is in a rural area (ie somewhat isolated) you may find that difficult to insure in the UK. What insurers prefer to deal with is property in locations they are familiar with so if you own rural property you may have to make arrangements with a local insurer.

If you are taking your valuables or money abroad with you, then check carefully with your home insurance company to see exactly what type of insurance you are covered for. It's best to have an all risks policy but do bear in mind that an all risks policy will cover you for accidental loss – it won't cover you if you've been deliberately careless. If your camera is stolen then you are covered – if your camera is stolen because you've left it on a crowded beach whilst you go for a swim, then don't expect your insurance company to be too sympathetic.

Do take care when making a claim as your insurance company will require a certificate from the police before settling a claim resulting from criminal activity. You must tell the police the value of everything that you have lost and they will write it into the certificate. You must be ready with these figures before you go and see the police.

Criminality

Those people who came to Portugal in the early 70s are sure to remember that you could leave your house unlocked or leave your car open on the street all night. Unfortunately, Portugal is like every other country in western Europe and has seen a significant increase in crime against property. Although part of the problem can be put down to unemployment in some areas, it's also an unfortunate reflection of increasing drug abuse. In the last few years, the amount of crime resulting from drugs and the relentless trafficking of drugs along the south coast has been on the increase.

This is something which the property owner cannot afford to ignore and it's a fact that must be taken into consideration when deciding where and what property to buy. If you are not going to be living permanently in your home, you should be careful when buying in an isolated location. Many isolated houses are broken into during the owner's long absences and even while they are staying in them. If you are going to be away for long periods, it makes sense to buy a house in an area where someone can keep a watchful eye on it.

Be on your guard

It's often the case that break-ins and robberies in holiday homes occur when the property is occupied but when the family have just gone out for a while to the shops or to a restaurant. Criminals seem to expect that there will be money in the house when people are living there. And it is cash, or valuables that can be turned into cash they are after. Your furniture and clothes are normally of little interest.

Break-ins also often occur as soon as people arrive on holiday. It's at that time that you have a fair amount of cash on you and it's also at a time when you are least on your guard. So, as a tip, take extra special care when you first arrive in Portugal on holiday. Lock your valuables and cash away and make sure that all the doors and windows are locked when you go out for that first restaurant meal.

Home security

When buying your home or having one built, it makes sense to think about its security. One of the simplest solutions is to have metal grilles across all the windows and also to have special metal grille doors as well as wooden doors. Wherever possible, have double locks for additional security and make sure that all the windows can be well secured from inside the house. Sophisticated modern security systems are now currently available in Portugal.

Install a safe

It could be well worth your while installing a safe somewhere inside the house. If you are using your home for a holiday, you are going to have to bring passports with you, credit cards, tickets, cash, travellers cheques and so on and it can be a problem keeping all this secure if you don't have the correct facilities. Installing a safe isn't very difficult and it can save a lot of unnecessary carrying around of valuables. Think carefully about the jewellery you take on holiday – it's far easier to leave it at home in the security of your own bank and it isn't absolutely essential to take your best watch and rings with you if all you are looking for is three weeks in the sun.

10 Timesharing

If you go to Portugal and have a thoroughly enjoyable two weeks' holiday, then that can be a very good reason for going to Portugal again and having another thoroughly enjoyable two weeks' holiday. It isn't a good reason for going through all the problems of buying a property in order to have a place of your own for two weeks a year.

So, an early decision has to be whether or not buying property is really worthwhile. The annual cost of even a small property in Portugal (including the interest you lose on the money you have used to purchase the property) will almost certainly be more than the cost of a two week holiday. If you only need your own property for the freedom that it gives you, then renting a villa could be a far cheaper option.

If, on the other hand, you can get out to Portugal two or three times a year or if other members of your family can put it to good use when you don't need it, then the idea of a second home might look a lot more attractive. And there's no doubt that having a familiar base in Portugal where you can 'do your own thing' is often the starting point for an ideal holiday. For many people, timesharing is the perfect compromise.

The principle

The principle of timesharing is simple enough:

- A developer builds a number of units in a single

development which could be a series of individual houses or a block of apartments.
- Rather than buy a unit outright, you purchase the right to use the property for a specified period each year for a specified number of years or indefinitely.
- The right of use is an asset which you can sell or, if the timeshare is affiliated to one of the exchange organisations, you can exchange it for a similar right in another property even in another country. You may also let other people use the property if you are unable to use it yourself during your particular time period.
- All the annual costs of running the complete property are paid for by a management company, set up by the developer, and you will be charged an annual management fee to cover all these costs.

In principle, therefore, timesharing can be a relatively inexpensive way of purchasing a share in a property with exclusive rights to use it at a given time. Some people use this principle to vary their holidays throughout the year and buy timeshares in two or three properties. It can be a very effective method of providing yourself with a holiday base without the overall problems of actually owning a property.

Do bear in mind, though, that it is not a direct comparison with, say, a packaged holiday:

- You still have to pay for the flight.
- You have tied up capital.
- Management costs may be high.
- Resale could be difficult.

The authorities in Portugal also take a close interest in timesharing and the Portuguese National Tourist Office publishes literature promoting the timesharing industry. The official view is that it stimulates domestic tourism by offering guaranteed accommodation at reasonable cost and will encourage people living outside Portugal to bring foreign currency into Portugal and to invest it there.

The pressure to buy

However, like everything in life, timesharing is not entirely
without its problems. The first of these is a simple matter
of mathematics. By selling the future use of a property, the
developer recovers his initial cost very quickly and makes a
tidy profit as well. He retains the ownership of the overall
property itself so he has both sold it and kept it. All the
future costs of running the property are taken care of by the
management fee and the end result is a rather lucrative
business for the developer. All you then need is for a number
of developers to realise the potential of timesharing and you
have the ideal breeding ground for problems. The lure of a
home in the sun to the buyer with a prospect of quick profits
to the seller leads immediately to the formation of a high
pressure sales team with the end result that timesharing –
and the timesharing companies – now have a dreadful
reputation in Spain and Portugal.

Holidaymakers, particularly on the Algarve, have been
literally plagued by timeshare salespeople who have pestered
them to attend timeshare exhibitions. Once there, the pressure
to commit yourself to the purchase of a two week timeshare
is intense with all kinds of inducements being offered to
would-be purchasers. The position has got so bad that the
Office of Fair Trading in London has produced a series of
guidelines to people contemplating buying a timeshare:

* Sign nothing during your first meeting with the salesman
  unless you are given a written guarantee that you have
  the right to change your mind within a reasonable period
  of time.
* Pay nothing, not even a small deposit, at the first meeting
  unless you're completely sure you want to go ahead (and
  unless the deposit is refundable if you change your mind
  within a reasonable period of time).
* Beware of any pressure put on you to sign at once to
  obtain a discount or other benefit.
* Beware of gifts and prizes which may be designed to

encourage you to visit the site or to buy within a
deadline.

- Insist on full details in writing of what you're being
  offered. These details should include:

  — The full price.
  — The type of tenure you will have.
  — How you are to pay for it (including interest rates).
  — A copy of the contract.
  — Any additional terms or conditions.
  — Information on what will happen at the end of the
    timeshare.

- Take your time considering the offer. You should read
  the contract and get independent advice from your
  solicitor in the UK.
- Ask about maintenance charges. They're likely to go up
  after you have bought so check what is planned, what
  the charges include and how the increases are to be
  decided and by whom.
- Find out if there is an owner's association to represent
  your interests. You should find out what power they
  have over the management company and what say you
  will have in the management arrangements.
- Finally, make sure you really can afford what you are
  about to buy and don't think of a timeshare as an
  investment in the same way as buying a house or flat as
  your permanent home.

There are, of course, a number of perfectly ethical developers
in the timeshare market. They have been seriously troubled
by the tactics that have been used by other companies and
they have formed the Timeshare Developers Association.

Members of the Association operate a five day cooling-off
period and are obliged to follow the requirements of a code of
conduct. The Association has also produced its own leaflet
(available from the Association's offices at 23, Buckingham
Gate, London SW1E 6LB telephone 01–921 8845) which
highlights some questions you should ask:

- Is the timeshare part of an exchange organisation?
- Is there a cooling-off period?
- Are there any penalties if you decide not to go ahead?
- Is there an association of names?

Perhaps the most important advice they give you is to regard a timeshare as an investment in **holidays** and not to regard it as an investment in property.

General considerations

There are two aspects of timesharing that you need to examine:

1 What rights does Portuguese law give you as a timeshare owner?
2 What rights do you have under the timeshare agreement with the timeshare company?

As far as the second point is concerned, it is up to you to take as much care as you can when buying your timeshare in much the same way as you would with any other kind of agreement.

So what should you be aware of? Irrespective of the legal vehicle used for creating the timeshare, the most important points to take note of are:

- Exactly what rights are you buying?
- What will happen in the future?

As a first step, you must make sure you fully understand all the details of what you are buying. The following checklist is by no means exhaustive but it will give you an idea of the sort of thing to look out for in the purchasing contract:

- Who actually owns the property?

- Is the time period guaranteed?
- Can you let other people use the property?
- Can you sub-let the property?
- Are there any restrictions on sub-letting?
- What restrictions are there on selling the timeshare?
- What facilities can you use?
- Are they free?
- Do you have to retain the timeshare for a minimum number of years?
- What happens if you die? Can you bequeath the timeshare in your Will?
- Can you exchange your time period for a similar time period in another property?
- How is the management fee calculated?
- Are there any hidden extras?
- What are the rules for increasing the fee in the future?

Think of the future

It is important also to understand that timeshare is for a long time. However, although you may have bought the right to use the property, the property still belongs to the developer. He is running a business and businesses are bought and sold. You could find that at some time in the future, your developer sells out and you come under the control of a different management group. They may have different ideas as to what constitutes good management and, with the development profits all gone, they may be relying on the management fee to provide their future reward.

When buying your timeshare, therefore, do think carefully about what might happen in the future. Your safest option is to buy through reputable and financially secure companies but even that is no guarantee that the property you have a timeshare in is going to stay with that developer. There's also no guarantee that developer is going to stay independent because he may be bought out by another, larger developer.

The legal position

Timesharing in Portugal enjoys legal rights which are not available to timeshare owners in, say, Spain. In Spain, although the law is able to recognise ownership of an asset (eg an apartment), it is not able to recognise ownership of that asset for a period of time. Portuguese law, on the other hand, is able to make this distinction and is able therefore to give the timeshare owner significantly greater protection than under Spanish law.

At the time of going to print a new timeshare law was passed in Portugal. However, as it has not yet been published by the Portuguese Government, it has not been possible to incorporate the changes in this edition of 'Your Home In Portugal'. The current law (which was passed in 1981) created a new right in the area of real estate – the right to the ownership of the property for a stated period of time (known as the 'right of periodic habitation'). This provides better legal protection for holders of holiday timeshares which up to 1981 they had only had through the legal protection given to them contractually by the timeshare company.

Timesharing in Portugal is therefore what is known as a 'minor right in realty' – it can be recorded as belonging to you in the land registry and it is a right which can be bought and sold. However, it is only the right of **occupation** which belongs to you – the ownership of the property itself (for example, a block of apartments) still belongs to the registered owner of the block. Indeed, there is a clause within the law which says that the owner can buy and sell the property without the timeshare rights being affected in any way at all.

Who are the owners?

What is important is that you understand the distinction between the registered **owner** of the block and the **timeshare**

or marketing company. They may be one and the same but it would not be unusual for you to be dealing with the timeshare company who are marketing the timeshares on behalf of the owners. Your rights are those that you have in respect of the **owners** not necessarily the timeshare company. It is not unknown for timeshare companies to fail to account for deposits paid to them – as a result the owners have refused to recognise the purchase of the units or to refund any money paid out.

The owners of the property are bound to provide the services and rights of occupation which you are entitled to by virtue of owning your timeshare. Anybody taking over the ownership of the property (which could be another buyer or could be a bank foreclosing on the mortgage) also takes on board the responsibility to provide you with all the services that you are entitled to under the timeshare agreement. If they were to fail to provide the services, you would have the right to sue them. The law in fact goes even further than this – timeshare owners **cannot** organise themselves together to arrange for the necessary level of management services and pay for them. The responsibility is the registered owners' and the only right you have is to claim against them.

The deeds

A pre-condition of using the property for timeshare is that it must have been defined as being for tourist purposes only (known as a classification of touristic utility). This classification is given by the Ministry of Tourism in conjunction with the local authority. Also, because most timesharing properties are apartments, the necessary steps must have been taken to create a deed of horizontal property (see chapter 7). Once these have been drawn up, then the timeshare title can be effected before a notary.

The deed constituting the periodical right of habitation will of course first have to be registered at the land registry in order to create a legal title to the individual timeshare units.

Consequently, if the owners have not registered the timeshare deed, then there will be a delay in issuing the land registry certificates to the individual timeshare owners. The delay is usually caused either because the developers suddenly realise the cost of the exercise or because of the land registry taking a long time to create the, often, hundreds of new titles that are bound to arise for a timeshare development.

The deed lodged with the land registry has to contain a certain amount of information about what rights you have and what rights the company has. It must for example include the following information:

- The dates on which each period of occupancy starts and finishes.
- The rights of timeshare owners, particularly in relation to the **communal** parts of the complex.
- The obligations of the timeshare owner to pay for the timeshare and to pay the management fees.
- The responsibilities of the owners relating to the furnishing and equipment of the property together with such things as cleaning and maintenance.
- The rules for compensation if any part of the complex is damaged or destroyed.

In this way, the rights and obligations of both are incorporated into the deed and are therefore enforceable by law. However, it is up to you to check the deed.

The law also provides for timeshare rights to be in perpetuity and if there's nothing in the deeds to the contrary, that is what you have. However, most owners will take the other legal opportunity open to them and that is to restrict your timeshare rights to a minimum of 20 years.

Selling your timeshare

Your legal title to your timeshare is issued by the land registry. This is like any other title to property and it's something which can be bought and sold. Consequently, if you sub-let your property or sell it to somebody else, then there is nothing in law to prevent your doing this (although it would be within the owners' rights for them to ask that they are notified of the change of ownership). All the rights which you currently enjoy under the timeshare would automatically pass to the new timeshare owner and any clauses in any agreement which reduced the rights of the new timeshare owner would be unenforceable in law.

One important point to note is that there is nothing in law that requires you to automatically offer the owners the first refusal on a re-sale (although there is nothing in law that would prevent the owners putting a clause in the agreement that asks you to offer them the first refusal on re-sale). If this condition is in the contract, then obviously you are obliged to follow it but there is nothing in law that says you must accept the price you are offered. The law merely requires you to notify the owners and ask whether or not they wish to have first refusal on your timeshare – if they don't (or if they offer you too low a price), then you are perfectly free to go and sell your timeshare on the open market.

By and large, in order to comply with the law, all that you are required to do is to abide by the terms of the agreement and to take what is called a 'passive' role. The owners on the other hand have to take an active role in the management of the complex to make quite sure that it is kept in good condition and well maintained so that you and the other timeshare owners are able to enjoy the property in the way that was originally intended.

The management fees

The final part of the law deals with the regular payments that you are obliged to make to the owners. Clearly, your future outgoings are not going to be something which can be fixed with any great certainty for any period of time (given inflation and other factors) but the basis on which these regular payments can be increased will almost certainly be incorporated in the deeds and will be related to a fixed scale, ie the retail price index in Portugal. In some cases, the deed also allows for these fees to be 'commuted' to a lump sum payment which then relieves you of the obligation to pay them in the future. Clearly, the owners are going to take a very cautious view of this and the sum is likely to be a very large one to compensate them for a possibly high rate of inflation in the future.

As with all agreements, you'll be expected to meet your regular payments on time (and there's even a provision within the law that will enable the owners to demand payment again if you sub-let your timeshare to a third party. Naturally, they'll be obliged to refund to you any payments that you make as well but the right to demand payment from a third party in advance of any payments from you is guaranteed by law). You will probably find that your timeshare deed explicitly states that your rights to ownership can only be exercised if your fees are up to date.

11 Letting your property

There are two ways in which you can let property that you own in Portugal:

1 You can let your property to people for an extended period of time, ie they regard it as their temporary home for several months.
2 You can let your property for short periods of time ie for holidays.

Use as a temporary home

Under these circumstances, you will be allowing people to use your property for an extended period of time and so it is important that you make it clear from the start the basis on which the property is to be made available. The risk you run is that a loosely worded agreement could be interpreted as something other than temporary in which case your tenant obtains much more protection under the law. Most important from your point of view is that it would then become quite difficult to remove the tenant and for you to repossess your property.

Consequently, if you are considering long-term letting of your property it is important to engage the services of a solicitor or a specialised estate agent to get the agreement correctly drafted. The contract should at least contain a clause that expressly states that the letting is a temporary arrangement for holiday purposes only.

It would be wise to ensure that your property is furnished (in which case you should prepare a full list of contents to be signed by your tenant). Letting an unfurnished house weakens your position in the event of a dispute as a judge may rule that an unfurnished dwelling cannot by definition be a temporary dwelling. To make quite sure that the position is clear, the contract should stipulate a total rent and then break this down into the proportion allocated to renting the property and the proportion allocated to renting the contents.

Obviously, you should choose your tenant with great care. The nuisance value of a bad tenant cannot be compensated for no matter how good the rent you are obtaining. Get as many references as you can about your prospective tenant, particularly a reference from his bank. If you are dealing with the letting yourself and not through an agent, then you will naturally wish to meet your prospective tenant and make up your own mind.

Long-term letting of your Portuguese property is no different from long-term letting of any other kind of property. There are dangers and it's up to you to take every possible precaution you can to make sure you're letting it to the right kind of people and that they fully understand that it is your property which at some point in the future you are going to want back.

The only two types of preventive contracts under which you can effectively evict an unwanted tenant are as follows:

1 Contracts for rental of residential property for short periods in coastal towns or other tourist areas, or for special and, by their very nature, temporary purposes.
2 Contracts for the rental of property normally lived in by the landlord where the property is being rented for a specific period and is only available because of the temporary absence of the landlord.

Short-term letting

Many people buy property in Portugal for their own holidays
and then set out to cover some of their costs by letting it
out for holiday use when they don't need it. If you have a
wide circle of friends and relations you may well be able to
arrange this yourself but this has the disadvantage that you
are dependent on people's goodwill to keep the property in
good condition and to leave it clean and ready for the next
occupant. Unless you can come to some arrangement with a
neighbour in Portugal to keep an eye on the property, you
can anticipate some problems with people returning from
holiday and complaining about broken lightbulbs, electrical
equipment not working, etc.

The alternative is to hand the job over to a letting agent who
will do everything for you, including routine domestic
maintenance. The rents will be set by the agency and after
deducting their costs they will pay the balance to you. The
amount you can expect to receive will be written into an
agreement but you are unlikely to get guarantees of income
other than for a purely nominal amount. Under these
circumstances you need to be reassured that the agents have
a good administration because in addition to their normal
duties they will also, in the case of an ad hoc contract, have
to prepare invoices for the rentals on a monthly basis. Since
agents generally require you to deposit with them a fairly
substantial sum of money to keep them going during the
season it is essential that the invoices get sent out regularly
so that you do not have cashflow problems.

You can also employ an agent simply to maintain the property
under an arrangement which will also require them to check
the inventory periodically, pay the maid, pay the bills and so
on. In the Algarve this is generally known as 'villa
management' and agents will charge you a management fee
and either a percentage of the letting contract or handling
fee for each tenant, with all their costs on top.

Also, make sure there are no clauses in the purchase contract or in the title deeds which restrict your right to let the property. In some cases, you may find that you have to use the services of the building promoter's letting agency.

If a property is situated in a development which has the official classification of touristic utility (*utilidade turística*) then there may be legal restrictions on your ability to let the property independently. If a development has at least 100 beds then the law states that such a development must be maintained by one entity, ie a management company whose job it will be to ensure that the development is properly maintained and doesn't get run down. The inducement to the company is that they are given the legal right to let the properties which are situated on the estate they manage.

However the law is not designed to protect a bad management company and if the owners are dissatisfied with the service then they can club together and dismiss the management company and appoint somebody else. Also, although the management company must by law give details of all the expenditure incurred in letting and maintaining property they are not bound to give details of the income they have received.

Choosing a local letting agency

If you choose a local letting agency, do so with great care. The majority are perfectly respectable and will treat you with honesty. Others are less than honest and will rely on the fact that you may probably be (literally) a thousand miles away and unable to check up on them.

By and large, you have to investigate the agencies which are offering their services and make your own judgment. The following guidelines may be helpful:

• Ask for references from satisfied users and go and see them (or write to them) and ask for confirmation of their satisfaction. If the agency is unwilling to provide the names of satisfied clients, find another agency. And make sure the clients are based in the UK, not in Portugal.

- Use well established companies and attempt to get some background information on their financial stability. Choose companies that have been operating for some time.
- Don't believe wildly optimistic figures of potential income. Get some brochures in the UK on the costs of renting holiday property in the area so you can get an idea of the likely weekly income that the agency will be receiving during the peak holiday periods.
- Don't believe promises that your property will be occupied all the time that you're not there. There is an over supply of available accommodation and although you may get 100% occupation during the peak holiday periods, you can expect lower than that during the off-peak season.
- Don't accept a percentage of the net rental income that is less than 60–75%. Make sure you receive payment as soon as the letting period has ended and don't be prepared to sit and wait for the agency to settle their account.
- Ask for evidence that the agency have paid your tax deductions to the authorities. As from 1 January 1989, agents and tour operators letting properties owned by non-resident foreigners are required to deduct 16% withholding tax from all income derived from letting and account for it to the Portuguese Revenue.
- Check the position from time to time. Ask the agency for a regular schedule of lettings and then get a neighbour to check the property during periods when the property is apparently un-let.

With a good agent, you can expect a reasonable flow of income from your property. But don't be too ambitious – if you end up covering your running costs, you will have done well.

Letting through tour operators

Apart from short-term letting via local agents it is often worthwhile to let your property direct through one of the tour operators (particularly if you have a villa as there are agencies who specialise in this type of property). Tour operators will generally have their own management team in the area where your property is situated and may often take on the management of the property itself, providing maids and so on.

Contracts for guaranteed income can be obtained from tour operators and these will generally be calculated at a lower daily rate than if a contract is simply on an ad hoc basis. If you need to rely on rental income it is probably best to go for a guaranteed contract. All contracts with tour operators are negotiated at least a year in advance of the season concerned. In other words, you need to start looking for a contract round about June or July for the following summer and round October or November for the following winter. Tour contracts tend to cover two seasons, one beginning 1 April and generally ending middle of October, the other beginning around 1 November and ending on 30 March. Rates on ad hoc contracts will generally cover three seasons: a low season, a mid season and a high season. You can expect to get about as much as twice the amount of a low season daily rate during the high season.

Rates may also be simply calculated on a daily basis irrespective of the number of tenants and the property or may vary according to how many tenants actually occupy the property on any given day. On a guaranteed income contract it is usual to obtain a deposit early in the season ie January or February for the summer season when you will receive your money in stage payments.

Letting through tour operators does however have its drawbacks. For example you will almost certainly not be able to use the property during the contracted period. Also if you then decide to sell the property whilst it is still rented you will have to ensure that possession of the property is only given after the contract has ended or get your purchaser to agree that he will honour the rental contract. In this instance, he will obviously be entitled to receive the income after completion. Failure to adhere to any contract will undoubtedly result in a fairly hefty bill and/or legal proceedings by the tour operator.

12 Selling your property

Advance preparation

When buying a property in Portugal you should always keep in mind the possibility that one day you might want to sell it again. You might find out that after some time you're just not cut out for life in Portugal or that you can't use the property enough to justify its costs. On the other hand, you might be enjoying life in Portugal so much that you now want to buy a different type of property having had a chance to look around for what really suits you.

The things to keep in mind at the time of purchase so that your property can be sold easily at a later date are:

1 Make sure that you've tied up all the legal loose ends and that you have good title to your property.
2 Make sure that your *escritura* has all the necessary import licences attached to it so that you don't have any problems in exporting the proceeds. Make sure that the money that you imported into Portugal to buy your property was correctly credited to your import licence otherwise it might cause you problems later on.
3 Keep your property maintained and attractive looking. Some specialist organisations are now offering to keep properties in good decorative order for a fixed annual sum. If you're not able to maintain your home without help, this kind of service can help you and can also maintain the value of an expensive asset.

Chapter 13 contains details of capital gains tax on the sale of individual private dwellings including building land.

Methods of selling

Private sales

One of the first decisions you must make when you come to sell your house is whether to use an agent or to undertake all the work yourself, which as an owner you are quite entitled to do. It is also possible to give power of attorney (a *procuracao*) to another private person to sell a property on your behalf. You do this before a notary (which may be at a Portuguese Consulate abroad if you wish), and the cost is normally quite small.

Sales through agents in Portugal

If you ask an estate agent to sell your house, remember that only registered real estate agents are legally allowed to sell on your behalf. By law, they can charge any percentage on the sale that they are able to negotiate with you and they will usually ask you to sign a form which specifies this commission. It will usually be at least 5%.

It's worthwhile taking care when signing this form because built into it (occasionally on the reverse side) may be a clause which gives them an exclusive right to sell on your behalf. If you decide to accept such a clause, you will be liable to pay the agent the agreed commission even if you sell your house without his help.

If you decide to give an agent an exclusive agreement then it is normally set for a fixed period during which you may **not** withdraw. You can of course negotiate the fixed period and normally three to six months should be enough time to entrust the sale to one agent.

The important thing to ensure with an estate agent is exactly what the commission will include, eg will it include any advertising that they may do. Also, you must agree with the agent exactly when the commission is payable. Where the contract provides for payment of a property in stages then the agent may request that the commission is payable out of the first payment. This should be strongly resisted. It is always best to pay the agent at completion but, failing that, you should arrange that he receives his commission in stages at the same time and in the same proportions as the stage payments. You must also agree with the agent that in the event of a purchaser defaulting, the agent also loses his deposit or fee.

You must also stipulate that any payments to be made under the contract must be paid directly to you. If payments are channelled through the agent, you should not sign the contract until you have received payment of the deposit.

Sales through overseas agents

It is perfectly legal for you to sell your property through an agent whose business is conducted outside Portugal provided that the agent restricts himself to looking for buyers outside Portugal. Once again, the commission charged is a subject of negotiation between you and the agent. In some cases, your agent may offer to accept payments in foreign currency from a potential buyer. There is nothing illegal in that provided that an import/export licence has been issued by the Bank of Portugal and that the payment is a deposit of not more than 10% of the purchase price. The very fact that the transaction is being conducted on an international scale between countries with different codes of conduct and different laws will make it harder for you to secure justice if your agent turns out to be less than honest or becomes insolvent.

It could be to your advantage to look for an agent who is a member of the Institute of Chartered Surveyors. If you have any problems then they have a code of practice which will enable you to have your complaints investigated.

13 The tax system

Introduction

There is nothing so certain in life as death and taxes – and
Portugal is no different in this respect from any other place.
This chapter is basically concerned with your tax liabilities as
a **homeowner**. It does not go into a great detail about the
complications of tax residence (although a limited
understanding is necessary, even for house purchase).

If you are thinking of moving permanently to Portugal then
it would be very much in your interests to get good specialist
advice on the implications of residence on your tax position.
This should be done **before** you leave the UK.

The taxes that the homeowner will be liable for in Portugal
fall into three principal groups:

1 The taxes that are paid as a result of buying a house.
2 The annual taxes that are paid as a result of owning (and
  perhaps letting) a house.
3 The taxes that are paid as a result of selling your property.

In addition, there is inheritance tax to think about if you die.

There will also be differences (principally in relation to the
annual taxes) depending on whether you are resident or non-
resident for **tax** purposes and this is explained in more detail
later on.

What taxes might you have to pay?

The total list of taxes that you could be liable for looks rather daunting, but there are no particular surprises in it. There are a number of 'obvious' ways in which you can be taxed as a homeowner and the Portuguese list is not that different from the UK list:

- If you buy property you may pay *Sisa*, a tax on conveyances.
- On building contracts you will have *IVA* (the Portuguese equivalent of VAT) to pay.
- When you have paid for your home, you will be liable for rates.
- If you let your home, you may have to pay income tax and withholding tax may be deducted at source if you are a non-resident.
- When you sell your property, you may have to pay capital gains tax.
- If you transfer your home (either by gift or through your Will) you may have to pay inheritance tax.

All these taxes are described in later sections.

Taxes on property

IVA is the Portuguese equivalent of VAT and was introduced when Portugal joined the Common Market on 1 January 1986. As in the UK, *IVA* is a tax which is levied on the supply of services, and property building is no exception. *IVA* is now applicable to building contracts and the rate is 17%. As the ultimate consumer, you are responsible for paying the tax so you should check that either the price quoted to you is inclusive of IVA or bear it in mind that it's going to be an additional cost at the end of the property purchase.

Sisa

At the time of publication, the passing of the new *Sisa* Law
was expected. The following contains the proposed changes
to this law as contained in the Bill before the Portuguese
Government and readers are advised to check whether any
further alterations have been made.

Sisa is a conveyancing tax which is payable on the transfer of
the rights to all or part of a property (not including fixtures
and fittings). *Sisa* applies not only to the purchase of property
but also to the purchase of leases on property in excess of
30 years and also to the transfer of shares in a company where
the shareholder obtains at least 75% of the share capital and
the company owns real estate.

The person liable for *Sisa* is the person named in the
promissory contract.

Sisa is generally charged on the value of the property being
transferred. However, you can reduce the amount of *Sisa*
that is chargeable by ensuring that your contract of purchase
and sale clearly identifies what part of the purchase price is
on account of fixtures and fittings, furniture or alterations to
the property itself.

Property subject to *Sisa* falls into three categories:

1 The transfer of rustic land which is charged at 8%.
2 Building and building land which is charged at 10%.
3 Residential property (if valued at over 15 million *escudos*)
   is charged at 10%.

If you buy a *quinta* (which involves the purchase of rustic
land and also the purchase of a building), then you will be
charged at 8% of the value of the land and 10% of the value
of the building.

There are a number of exemptions from *Sisa* the most
common being:

- Transfers of residential property under 5 million *escudos* are exempt from *Sisa* and there is a sliding scale of *Sisa* on values between 5 million and 15 million *escudos*.
- If you are buying a property for permanent residence, then *Sisa* is not charged if the value of the property does not exceed 10 million *escudos*. (Exemption only effective till 31 August 1989.)

If you are claiming exemption from *Sisa* on the basis that the property you are acquiring is for your permanent residence, then there are certain limitations which you must bear in mind:

- You must take up permanent residence in the property within six months of buying it.
- You must buy the property with the intention of living in it for at least six years (although you would not be required to fulfil this obligation in the event of the death of a member of your close family).
- The exemption will be lost if you acquire a **second** property and claim exemption for that.

An application for exemption has to be lodged with the tax department who will issue you with the appropriate form. You will also need to declare that you have not previously claimed exemption from *Sisa*.

The good news for timeshare owners is that no *Sisa* is payable when you purchase a timeshare.

The payment of *Sisa*

Sisa is usually payable immediately before the act which confers the property to you (ie the making of the *escritura*). Once your import licence has been issued you will soon receive notice to complete in accordance with the terms of your contract. You will need to go to the Tax Department where the property is situated (*reparticao de financas*) taking with you a copy of your contract and your cheque book! If the purchase price is stated in foreign currency, the Tax Department will convert this into *escudos* in accordance with the official rate of exchange. There will be other forms to fill in but the Tax Department will normally do this for you.

If you are buying a building plot, then the documentation supporting the payment of *Sisa* will have to mention this fact. You will also need to ensure that the amount that is being declared as the value of the land is in fact the value which the tax department has allocated to the land. This is because the tax department will themselves have valued the land for *Sisa* purposes and they may not agree with the declared value on which you have paid *Sisa*. You may then find that despite having originally paid your *Sisa* and even completed on the property, the tax department inform you of **their** valuation, giving you 15 days to pay the extra *Sisa*. Failure to pay results in interest being charged on the amount of outstanding tax.

If this happens to you, then the law enables you to appeal by requesting a second valuation of the property. However, it would be sensible to consult the developer first because they may have had a recent revaluation carried out on all their plots. There's nothing unusual in appeals against valuations – developers would normally do it because it affects the *Sisa* that you pay and also the capital gains which the developers are liable to pay on the sale of building plots. Although more unusual, the same may occur when buying a resale residential property.

If you effect the *escritura* abroad (ie in a Portuguese Consulate General or elsewhere), *Sisa* is payable within 180 days of the legal transfer of the property to you. On the other hand, if you take possession of a property **before** the *escritura* is effected, then you will be liable to pay the *Sisa* immediately.

The value on which the tax is payable

Previously, part of the accepted tax evasion in Portugal was to declare a small value in your title deed. That meant that the

amount of money actually required to be brought into
Portugal for buying the property was less than the real
purchase price meaning that a sizeable proportion of the
purchase price remained abroad. This effectively meant that
it was a way of the seller getting money out of the country
(ie by-passing Portugal's exchange control laws) and
reducing his capital gains tax (ie evading his own tax
liabilities). Now, since 1 January 1989, if you go along with
the seller's wishes, **you** will land yourself with an enormous
income tax bill when you sell the property.

Overall, by signing an agreement where the declared value is
less than the true value (with the inducement that you will
be paying a lower amount of *Sisa* or no *Sisa* at all), you are
breaking the law. The Bank of Portugal is regularly supplied
with tables of land and property values from the various tax
departments and the value declared in each application is
carefully checked against these. If the price of the property
declared in the application is considered to be substantially
lower than the real market value, then you may find it difficult
to get permission to import the currency.

In addition, you could find yourself in trouble with the tax
authorities. If they consider that the low value is a **deliberate**
under-declaration then not only will you have to pay the
excess *Sisa*, you will also be liable to a fine equal to twice
the total amount of *Sisa*. It may be sometime before the tax
department catches up with you (long after you've effectively
bought the property) so you could find yourself with a nasty
surprise.

This point cannot be stressed too strongly. It's one where you
may be advised by the 'old hands' to declare a low value
because that is the way things are done in Portugal. They are
behind the times. For example, suppose you purchase a new
property for 20m *escudos* and declare 14m *escudos* in order to
avoid *Sisa*:

1　14m *escudos* will be on the import licence application.
2　The declared purchase price is 14m *escudos* as well.

What happens next is that the tax department find out about the under-declaration and they realise that you are trying to evade tax on 20m *escudos*. Not only will they ask you for the tax on 20m *escudos* (2,000,000 *escudos*), they will also fine you twice that amount and give you 15 days to pay the lot, ie a total bill of 6,000,000 *escudos*.

The moral is – don't under-declare values and be prepared to pay your full taxes.

The annual taxes – the 1989 Portuguese tax reforms

There is nothing particularly complicated about working out which Portuguese taxes you are going to be liable for. Portugal has two principal forms of annual taxation affecting the property owner – a municipal tax and an income tax. Most people regardless of whether they are resident in Portugal or not will have to make some kind of tax declaration every year.

Decree Law 442–A/88 of 30 November 1988 introduced a new income tax code called IRS (*Imposto Sobre o Rendimento das Pessoas Singulares*). This code, which came into force on 1 January 1989, introduces, in a similar way to the UK, a single tax on income. Tax may be charged on income derived from the following sources which are categorised into nine schedules:

A – Employment
B – Self-employment from scientific and professional activities
C – Commercial and industrial income including tourism and property management
D – Agricultural and farming
E – Capital (excluding interest from deposits)

F – Income from property (including rental income)
G – Capital gains
H – Pensions
I – Other income.

The tax bands

Taxes are charged in bands as follows:

TABLE A

Band	Percentage Rates	
(000's *escudos*)	Normal (A)	Medium (B)
Up to 450	16	16
450–850	20	17.882
850–1,250	27.5	20.960
1,250–3,000	35	29.150
Over 3,000	40	–

The method of tax calculation is to take the tax band immediately **below** that applicable to your taxable income and apply the rate applicable in the medium (B) column. The excess is charged at the next higher rate band at the percentage rate in the normal (A) column.

For example, suppose you have a taxable income of 1,500,000 *escudos*. The tax band immediately below that income is the tax band applying to incomes of between 850,000 and 1,250,000 *escudos* for which the medium rate is 20.960%. This means that the first band of your income on 1,250,000 *escudos* is taxed at 20.96%.

The next 250,000 *escudos* is taxed at the next rate but at the normal rate ie at 35%.

Special rates of taxation and non-residents

a   Income of non-residents derived from schedules A and H is taxed at a rate of 25%

b   Interest accruing to current and deposit accounts is taxed at a rate of 20%

c   Income derived from other capital investments is taxed (in the case of non-residents) at a rate of 20%

d   Income from gains realised on the sale of personal property ie cars pictures etc is charged at 10%.

This is not a complete list as it only covers the taxes that are of principal interest to the property owner.

Resident or non-resident?

First though, let us clear up the business about whether you are resident or non-resident and remember it is important to distinguish between **tax** status and **immigration** status. In this chapter, we are dealing solely with residence for tax purposes; immigration status is covered in chapter 15.

Most countries in the world have broadly similar rules for determining tax residence, but we will start by looking at the UK regulations. You will be regarded as tax resident in the UK if:

* You spend 183 days or more per annum in the UK.
* You make habitual and substantial visits to the UK – visits are treated as habitual if they extend over a four year period and substantial if they last an average of three months (90 days or more) per annum when measured over that period.
* You make a visit to the UK, no matter how short the

duration, and you have accommodation (which could be just a room) available for your use.

This last point would appear to be a total catch-all but in fact it is waived for people in full-time gainful employment abroad. Nevertheless, it is an important consideration for the retired person.

Turning now to the Portuguese rules (and specifically article 16 of the IRS Code), you will be tax resident in Portugal in any year that you spend more than six months there (and, for this purpose, six months is defined as 183 days in any calendar year). You will also be regarded as a resident if you have a permanent abode in Portugal on 31 December of the tax year (ie you keep a house with the presumed intention of making it your home even if you spend less than 183 days there).

In both the UK and Portuguese residence rules 'year' means the tax year. However, in the UK, the tax year runs from 6 April to 5 April whereas in Portugal (as in most other countries of the world) the tax year is the same as the calendar year. The slightly different rules and periods means that it is perfectly possible for someone to be tax resident in both countries at once. This is not quite as bad as it sounds as there is a Double Taxation Agreement in force between Portugal and the UK which ensures, in essence, that tax is not levied twice on the same income (but at the same time sets out to ensure that the income is taxed at least once!). As from 1 January 1989 a non-resident must appoint a tax representative in Portugal whose job it is to ensure that all relevant returns are made.

The overall result for most people is that their tax status is determined by whether or not they have accommodation available to them in the UK or by the number of days a year they spend either in the UK or in Portugal. Immigration status (as explained in chapter 15) is determined by whether or not the Portuguese authorities are prepared to grant you residence status – they will take their taxes off you whether they like you or not!

In this chapter, we deal principally with the non-resident property owner although, where appropriate, we touch on the considerations for the resident property owner. In this case, the comments should be regarded as a guide and not as a substitute for specialist advice.

One particular area (which is beyond the scope of this book) is for people leaving England to live in Portugal. The precise day on which you leave the UK can have a significant impact on your tax bill and it's vital to take professional advice on that.

The new proposals

The UK rules described above relate to Inland Revenue law and practice as at December 1988 but it should be noted that this is currently under review. The Revenue issued a consultative document in July 1988 (Residents in the United Kingdom – the Scope of UK Taxation for Individuals) proposing a radical overhaul of the rules relating to the taxation of both Britons abroad and foreign nationals in the UK.

The proposals are complex and, of course, at this stage are just proposals – there is no indication of which proposals will be enacted or when. However, it is worth pointing out that the envisaged changes would be beneficial to British expatriates retired abroad. In effect, the amount of time that could be spent in the UK without becoming tax resident would be increased from an average of 90 days per annum to 120 days per annum and, more importantly, the 'visits with accommodation available' rule would be scrapped, thus enabling a Briton to keep a home in the UK without prejudicing his tax position.

This is good news, of course, but, for the time being, the

prudent individual will organise his affairs in accordance with current legislation – whilst perhaps looking expectantly to the future.

The taxes you may be liable to pay

The main annual taxes that affect people with property in Portugal are as follows:

- Income tax (including tax on pensions)
- Capital gains tax
- Property taxes

Income derived from property

This includes income derived from all types of property including land and any services arising from the letting of property. This would mean, for example, that if you let your property and charge extra for maid service, food provided etc, this income would also be chargeable. If you are a tenant and sub-let your property, then you would also be charged on the difference between the rent you pay to your landlord and the rent your sub-tenant pays you.

Deductions

Article 40 of the IRS Code allows deductions for the maintenance and conservation of your property.

a   Urban buildings

You are allowed to deduct 35% of your annual rental income for maintenance (15%) and conservation (20%). If your costs are higher than this, you may be able to deduct them by showing the relevant invoices to the Portuguese revenue provided they relate to electricity bills, rates, lift maintenance, cleaning, porterage, insurance, heating and air conditioning, property administration and condominium charges. Any repairs to the property may be deducted but you must keep the builder's receipts if they amount to more than 20% of your gross rental income.

b   Land and mixed properties (including *quintas*)

You can only deduct expenses relating to land maintenance and conservation provided you submit documentary evidence at the same time. If you own a *quinta*, you may deduct all allowable expenses in relation to the building (see above) but any expenses incurred in relation to your land will only be allowed if you are able to prove it by showing the appropriate receipts.

Pensions

For the pensioner, the position generally will be that your pension will be paid gross from the UK and will be subject to Portuguese income tax. This will apply to any form of retirement pension (your old age pension, pensions from any occupational schemes and also pensions from self-employed pension plans), invalidity or sickness pensions, maintenance payments and they will all be subject to tax whether they are temporary pensions or payable for life.

If you are receiving a Government pension (for example from the Civil Service or from the Armed Forces) then this will be paid net of UK withholding tax and there will be no further liability to Portuguese income tax under the Double Taxation Treaty.

No tax is charged on pensions which do not exceed 400,000 *escudos* a year. If your pension is more than 400,000 *escudos* but less than 1 million *escudos*, you will be entitled to an immediate deduction of 400,000 *escudos* and you will only be charged tax on half of the excess.

For example, if your pension is 900,000 *escudos*, you will only pay tax on:

900,000 – 400,000 ÷ 2 = 250,000 *escudos*.

Capital gains tax

Capital gains are all gains other than those which would be considered as commercial, industrial or agricultural, arising from:

— the transfer for value of any property or interests in real estate
— the transfer for value of shares in a company and any other personal property
— premiums acquired from the assigning of rental agreements or leases.

The tax therefore has an impact on the property owner and will arise when the property is sold.

The tax is due as soon as possession is given to the buyer. If you agree to give possession of your property to a buyer before the *escritura* is made, you will be liable to pay the tax charged on your gain on the date of possession. Article 17(1) of the code makes the tax payable by both residents and non-residents.

The capital gain becomes part of your income for the year in which it arises and is charged at half of the relevant rate in the relevant tax band.

If you acquired your property before 1 January 1989, whether in your name or in the name of a company, you will not be liable to pay tax on your gain. You will, however still have to pay capital gains tax on the sale of building land regardless of the date that you acquired it.

What is the basis for capital gains tax?

The tax is charged on the difference between the declared purchase price (for *Sisa* tax purposes) when you purchased your property and the price declared to the *financas* at the time of sale. If you under-declared your purchase price (thereby saving 10% *Sisa* on the undeclared amount) you could end up paying 20% tax on your gain. There is therefore little to be gained in under-declaring your purchase price.

If your purchase was exempt from *Sisa* then your property will be given the value which gave rise to the exemption ie 4,999,000 *escudos*.

If you were given the property or inherited it, the base value of the property will be taken as that declared for the payment of gift or inheritance tax (see later on in this chapter).

If you bought some land and later built a house on it, the base value of the property will be the value of the property for tax purposes (which you will find in your *caderneta predial*) or the total of the value of the land declared for *Sisa* tax purposes plus the costs of construction, duly documented, if this total is higher.

Capital gains and inflation

Provided that you have owned the property for at least 24 months, the amount of chargeable gain will be reduced by a fixed percentage (the co-efficient) which will be published annually by the Minister of Finance.

Allowable expenses and exemptions for reinvestment

You may deduct capital expenditure you have incurred during the last five years as well as expenses necessarily incurred for the sale of the property ie legal fees.

If you sell your property but reinvest the gains you have made within a period of 24 months in another residential property, or if you purchase a plot of land and build another residential property on it, the gain you have made will not be considered as chargeable income.

Property taxes

Until 1 January 1989, Portugal had a real estate tax called *contribuicao predial* which was a tax charged on the annual value of land and buildings whether you let the property or not. The tax often had an unfair effect because if you let your property one year and declared the income to the tax authorities, you would then be charged the same amount of tax the following year even if you had not let your property.

The new tax reform has abolished *contribuicao predial* and has introduced (by Decree Law 442–C/88 of 30 November 1988) a new tax called *contribuicao autarquica* or municipal tax. It is an annual tax payable to the local authority where your property is situated. It is payable in April or, if the amount of tax payable is more than 20,000 *escudos*, in two equal instalments in April and September.

Properties are divided into three categories for the purposes of taxation – rustic, mixed and urban. Urban properties are further divided into four classes: residential, commercial, building land and other.

The tax is payable by the registered owner or, where the property has not been registered, by the person in possession. There is a duty to register new properties for tax purposes within 90 days from the conclusion of building work. In the same way, if you make alterations or improvements to the property (ie build a swimming pool) the local Tax Department must be informed. The electrical, water and telephone authorities are not permitted to connect you to those services unless you have registered your property for tax purposes.

Interest is charged on all payments which are over a month late and, if you fail to pay altogether, the Tax Department may register a legal mortgage against your property which, in due time, could result in its sale at public auction.

In accordance with the new code, all properties are revalued every year for tax purposes. The basis for revaluation will in future be in accordance with rules contained in a new code, called the Valuation Code (*codigio das avaliacoes*). This code is yet to be published. Income derived from letting will in future be subject to income tax.

Rate of tax

> Rustic property – 0.8% of the tax value
> Urban property – 1.1% to 1.3% of the tax value

Mixed properties are charged at the rate of tax appropriate to the urban or rustic parts of the property.

Exemptions

Properties of national interest are exempt from municipal tax as well as certain residential properties acquired for the permanent abode of the taxpayer provided the following conditions are complied with:

— the taxable value of the property does not exceed 10 million *escudos*
— you take up possession of the property within 6 months of acquisition except for reasons beyond your control
— you live in the property for ten years.

Those property owners who were exempt from the old tax (*contribuicao predial*) should seek immediate professional advice as they may be affected by the new provisions.

Transitional provisions

a   The revaluation of properties

The values of many properties in Portugal have not been updated for a number of years and, as a result, the Portuguese legislature introduced a new law in September

1988 allowing for the revaluation of all properties as at 31 December 1988 as follows:

i   Urban Properties – 4% per year cumulative since the date of the last valuation up to a maximum of 100%
ii Rustic Properties – 20% per year cumulative since the date of the last valuation up to a maximum of 100%.

b   New valuations

Until the new valuation code comes into force, buildings will continue to be valued in accordance with the old *predial* tax code. Building land will be valued in accordance with the provisions of the *Sisa* and inheritance tax code.

c   Back taxes

Many local authorities are two or more years behind in sending out rate demands. It is envisaged that, with the introduction of the new tax reform, local authorities will quickly be getting up-to-date. Purchasers must ensure that proper provision is made to meet back payments and this will usually be done by withholding part of the purchase price and putting it on deposit.

Owners receiving demands for rates relating to previous years may pay these in three monthly instalments, providing the total sum exceeds 20,000 *escudos*.

Portuguese income tax returns

The Portuguese tax authorities are not very efficient in notifying you what your tax bill is, but are significantly more efficient when it comes to pursuing you for unpaid taxes. It's therefore important for you to take action to find if you are liable for income tax, when it has to be paid, where to get the forms, how much to pay and how to pay it. For this reason, it might be better to employ a local accountant familiar with the Portuguese tax system and ask him to do the job for you.

The Portuguese tax reforms introduced two separate forms for income tax returns:

— Form 1 (*Declaracao modelo 1*) when the taxpayer has only had income derived from the sources in schedules A and H (Employment and Pensions)
— Form 2 (*Declaracao modelo 2*) in all other cases.

Tax returns must be handed in to your local Tax Department by the end of February if you have had no income from sources in schedules B, C and D. In all other cases, you must hand in your tax return by 10 May in each year. Personal allowances in Portugal are minimal.

Payment of income tax

The Portuguese tax reforms have introduced a system of pay first and argue later. Income Tax must be paid by 10 May of each year in respect of income obtained in the previous year. In general, the tax must be paid at the same time as the tax return is handed in. The Tax Authorities are at liberty to review your tax calculations and will notify you of their assessment. You then have 30 days in which to appeal.

Under the Double Taxation Agreement between Portugal and the UK, you have to declare any gains you make on your UK Tax Return but you will get credit for the amount of Portuguese tax paid.

Inheritance tax

Inheritance tax is a tax that you must take into account, especially if you intend to live in Portugal. It does, however, apply to non-residents as well. Inheritance tax arises if you give assets away while you are alive or if you leave them to somebody in your Will. It is therefore **similar** to UK inheritance tax.

Who is liable to pay it?

- Inheritance tax is levied on the person receiving or inheriting the assets (the beneficiary).
- If you are resident in Portugal, then you are liable to inheritance tax on any assets given or bequeathed to you regardless of where they are situated.
- If you are non-resident then you are liable to Portuguese inheritance tax if you are given or are bequeathed assets that are situated in Portugal (and an obvious example is a house or apartment).

How is it calculated?

The calculation of the tax is complex but it is simple to follow in stages. The liability to inheritance tax is based on:

- The relationship between the giver and the receiver.
- The value of the gift or property.

By way of simple illustration, take the case of a retired couple of relatively modest means living in Portugal. If the husband dies, his widow could well have a small inheritance tax bill to pay. If, however, a wealthy widow were to leave her estate to her equally wealthy next door neighbour, the neighbour could face a substantial tax bill.

The relationship

There are four groups of relationship of the person receiving the gift:

Class I   – spouse and children under 21 (including adopted children).
Class II – other children and grandchildren.
Class III – parents and grandparents, brothers and sisters.
Class IV – other relatives and any non-relatives.

The value

The value of the gift for inheritance tax purposes is its **taxable value**. For most people, the major asset will be their home and the tax value (the *valor matricial*) is assessed at 15 times the annual letting value, as determined by the tax authorities. For assets which have no letting value (eg a car) the taxable value will be negotiated with the tax authorities.

Tax rates

			Class	
Value*	I %	II %	III %	IV %
1–250	–	4	10	30
250–500	8	10	16	38
500–1,000	13	16	23	46
1,000–5,000	18	21	29	53
5,000–10,000	23	26	36	60
10,000–50,000	33	36	49	76
50,000 +				
	* in '000s of *escudos*			

The calculation of the tax due is based on **two** tax bands only as follows:

● Find out in which band the highest rate applies and apply that rate as appropriate.

● The balance is charged at the next **lowest** band.

Example

> Mr and Mrs B, who are retired, own a villa with an estimated value
> of 10m *esc* and a rateable value of 120,000 *esc*. Mr B dies and leaves
> it to his wife who has no other assets in Portugal.
>
> *Calculation*
> 1   The relationship is Class I.
> 2   The value of the gift is 1.8m *esc* (ie 15 × 120,000 *esc*).
> 3   The tax rate on a gift of this value (for Class I) is 800,000 *esc* at
>   18% plus 13% on the remaining 1m *esc*.
> 4   The tax due is therefore 274,000 *escudos*.

The tax is payable over a period of three years, in six-monthly
instalments. If you pay in advance, you will get a discount
on any of the second and subsequent instalments which are
paid before the due date. By way of example, the discount
on the final instalment could be up to 30% if it is paid
immediately.

In the UK it is possible to give property to your wife free of
inheritance tax and to make limited gifts to your children in
a way which may avoid inheritance tax. **No such provisions
exist in Portugal**. If, therefore, you are planning to retire to
Portugal you need to think about the potential impact of
Portuguese inheritance tax and take competent financial
advice. The way you plan your investments and prepare things
in the event of your death are closely tied up with the way
you write your Will. It is advisable to write a Portuguese Will
if you have property in Portugal and this is dealt with in
more detail in the next chapter.

14 Making a Portuguese Will

Introduction

One of the most common problems in financial life in the UK is that so many people don't like making Wills. Quite why this should be so is not immediately obvious because it is basically so simple. One explanation might be that it's tempting fate to make a Will, but the reality is that it's tempting fate **not** to make one.

A Will is quite simply a statement of what **you** want to happen to your belongings when you die. If you don't leave instructions (which is known as dying 'intestate') then the law will have rules on how your property will be divided up amongst your surviving relatives. These rules may mean that your property is distributed in a way that you would most certainly not have approved of had you been alive. Consequently, writing a Will in the UK can save your family a considerable amount of trouble.

It isn't essential to use a solicitor for drawing up a Will but it's strongly advised that you should do so. Although you may have a very clear idea of how you wish your belongings to be divided up after your death, a solicitor will be able to draft your Will in terms that are completely unambiguous and that is the most important thing. The validity of your Will needs to be approved after your death and it's important then that there should be absolutely no misunderstandings at all about what you actually meant.

It is of course possible to incorporate your Portuguese assets into your English Will and that will be usually quite satisfactory. However, it will also be an extremely lengthy process to have your Will proved and that in turn will give your family problems. Having an English Will proved in England can take long enough (two years is not unknown) so it can be imagined just how long it will take to have an English Will proved in Portugal. If you've gone to the time and care to produce an English Will, it is no great problem to prepare a Portuguese Will for what will normally be fairly restricted assets in Portugal.

The position in Portugal

The position is exactly the same in Portugal. Writing a Portuguese Will is just as straightforward and dying without making a Will can cause your family considerable problems. You may have experienced problems grappling with the Portuguese legal system when you were buying your property. Consider what problems your family will have if they're trying to sort out problems after your death under circumstances which might make it very difficult for them to come to Portugal and sort the problems out in person. Writing a Will can save a tremendous amount of heartache for them and it doesn't take very long.

As with an English Will, it's not **obligatory** to use a lawyer to prepare your Will – you could just go and talk to your local notary. However, it will be very advantageous to do so. By discussing with a Portuguese lawyer exactly what you wish to happen to your property after your death, he will be able to take careful note of your wishes and advise you generally on how the Will should be expressed to carry out your true intentions under Portuguese law. Also, the Will may have to be written in Portuguese.

The form of your Will

In Portugal, you have the choice of making two types of Will. One is a 'public Will' which means that it will be written into the notarial books (in the same way as an *escritura*) and you will then be provided with legalised photocopies for your own records. The public Will will be written in Portuguese and signed in front of the notary in the presence of two witnesses. As with an *escritura* or any other official document effected in front of a notary, a translator will have to be present (if you cannot speak Portuguese) unless the notary can translate the document to you in English.

The alternative is to prepare a 'private Will' which is a handwritten document also signed before a notary and two witnesses. A private Will, however, is not written into the notarial books but will be handed back to you after the notary has approved it. He will do this by drawing up what is known as a *minuta de aprovacao* which testifies to the validity of the document.

A private Will may be written in English and may be in English form. This means that your solicitor in the UK could prepare a draft for you but you would then need to write it out in your own hand (as clearly as possible) and then take it to the notary in Portugal.

Drawing up your Will

Make sure that the lawyer incorporates a clause on the law of 'quick succession'. This is a common clause in English Wills and covers the case where both you and your spouse are, say, involved in a traffic accident. This ensures that if your spouse dies within, say, 30 days of your death, that the inheritance is set aside and that all your possessions are passed to the next in line to inherit. This then avoids inheritance tax having to be paid twice on the same assets.

If you have a Will in the UK, it is sensible to ensure that the wording in both Wills is such that they don't conflict.

Appointing executors

With a UK Will, it would not be at all unusual for you to appoint a member of your family as executor ie the person responsible for ensuring that your wishes are carried out. With Portuguese assets, and a Portuguese Will, this could be an unfair burden and therefore you should appoint a qualified executor. A Portuguese lawyer would be a good choice and it is important here to appoint him before your death and then name him in your Will, at the same time agreeing with him the fees that he will charge. If you name your bank or a non-Portuguese speaking solicitor as your executor they will almost certainly have to instruct a Portuguese lawyer after your death and his fees are then an open-ended expense which will be almost impossible to control.

Keep your heirs up-to-date

Make sure your UK solicitor is completely conversant with the contents of your Portuguese Will and make sure that he (and your heirs) know where to find a copy of it so that they can locate the notary who recorded it. If you have executed a private Will you should keep it in a safe place, eg your bank. It is also advisable to keep an up-to-date account of all your assets in Portugal – property, bank accounts, insurance policies etc.

Inheritance tax declarations and the payments of taxes in Portugal have to be made within a fairly short period after your death and your heirs should also be aware that inheritance tax and any other outstanding taxes must be paid before any change in the title can take place. There is nothing to prevent them from making a private sales contract but transfer of title can only take place after the inheritance has been accepted officially and the inheritance tax paid.

In the same way, you should tell your heirs exactly who your executor is so that they can make contact with him in the event of your death to help them in administering and distributing the inheritance. It would be sensible to keep a close eye on the likely level of inheritance tax that's due to be paid and to discuss with your heirs exactly how this money is to be raised if they don't want to sell the property that they are inheriting.

All in all, making a Portuguese Will is a sensible precaution to save your heirs any problems when you die. It's an entirely sensible aspect of financial planning and one which should be undertaken without any delay if you have purchased assets in Portugal. It's also sensible to prepare a Will in the UK and you should always keep your Wills up-to-date and reviewed regularly to take account of your changing financial and domestic circumstances.

15 Settling in

You have bought your property and now you are thinking of making it a more permanent arrangement, or perhaps of having a longer stay in Portugal. What you have to decide now is whether or not you are a tourist or a resident. It's important at this point to draw the distinction between being **legally** resident and resident for **tax purposes**. Chapter 13 explains the tax position and this is determined by rules outside your control. Your **legal** status in Portugal (ie whether you are a tourist or a resident) is to some extent a matter of choice but you cannot just become a resident – there are forms to fill in.

What you must understand, however, is that the two types of residence are different – you can **technically** be a tourist in Portugal but still be regarded as resident for tax purposes.

Tourist or resident?

The question of whether to stay in Portugal as a tourist or become a resident is a little vague in some areas. Basically, as a UK citizen, if you visit Portugal as a tourist you're allowed to remain there for 60 days without requiring a visa provided, of course, you have a valid passport to present to the authorities when you arrive in Portugal.

Tourist status has some advantages for people staying in Portugal for short periods. They are allowed to open certain types of bank accounts that residents can't open and also to drive a car on foreign plates for a limited period of time.

If you're going to make a temporary stay in Portugal (up to two months), then you don't need an entry visa provided you hold a British passport and you are classified as a British citizen. However, if you want to stay longer than that, then you will have to go to a foreigners' office in the area to apply for a 60 day extension. You will find a foreigners' office in all the major cities and towns in Portugal eg Lisbon, Oporto, Coimbra, Faro and so on. It's possible for you to obtain two such extensions (ie to make your maximum stay in Portugal up to six months in any calendar year after which you have to leave the country).

The route for anybody who wishes to remain in Portugal on a more permanent basis is to apply for a residence permit.

Applying for a residence visa

If you wish to apply for permanent residence then you will first need a visa. You should apply personally for this at the Portuguese Consulate General in London (or via an Honorary Consulate of Portugal in the UK) before coming to Portugal. The information that you will have to provide to the Consulate General is as follows:

- A completed and signed application form (V–2) (original plus two photocopies).
- Two passport photographs.
- Two copies of your passport (verified by a notary public or solicitor).
- Evidence of financial stability and declaration of why you wish to reside in Portugal.
- A medical certificate confirming your good health, translated into Portuguese and authenticated (original plus photocopy).

- A certificate obtained in Portugal to prove you have adequate housing arranged (original plus photocopy).

In addition to all the above documents, you will need further documentation to support your application depending on what you intend to do when you finally arrive in Portugal.

If you intend to work

- If you are taking up paid employment, then you will need written evidence from your future employer clearly showing that you have in fact been offered employment. You will also need the necessary approval of the Ministry of Labour to your working in Portugal.
- If you are self-employed, then you will need to be able to prove that you hold the necessary qualifications to exercise your profession in Portugal. You will also need to provide a copy of your import licence.
- If you're setting up in business on your own account, then you'll need written confirmation that you have been granted permission by the Foreign Investment Institute to set up your business. (If you haven't yet got that far, then you'll need to provide a copy of your import licence.)

If you are retired

If you're retired, you'll need to provide documentary proof of your retirement and to provide proof of the amount of your pension. You will also need confirmation from a Portuguese bank that you've opened an account in *escudos* in Portugal and you must also be able to prove that your monthly credit balance on this account is adequate to support you and your family.

People of independent means

If you are moving to Portugal to live and have the means to support yourself without working, then you'll need proof from a Portuguese bank that you've opened an account in *escudos* in Portugal and that the opening balance is not less than approximately £2,000 for you and each member of your family. If you intend to make a living through property investment you will need a legalised photocopy of the promissory contract relating to your property and a copy of the import licence.

When you submit these documents, you will receive a temporary slip of paper which is sufficient evidence of your residence application until the final card is issued. Separate applications are required for husband and wife and children over the age of 14.

It makes sense to apply for a visa in plenty of time because they can take at least eight months to be issued. Once your passport has been endorsed with the resident's visa, you then have permission to reside in Portugal.

Applying for permanent residence

You will still have to **fully** legalise your residence status (which will involve the completion of more forms) at the nearest office of the Ministry of Internal Affairs with a foreigners' department (*Servicos de Estrangeiros*) within 90 days of your arrival in Portugal. (The resident's visas which are granted to you by the Portuguese Consulate have a total validity of 120 days only.)

Once your application is successful, you will then be in possession of your *autorizacao de residencia*, the card that gives you the right to live in Portugal and to get the same consideration as a Portuguese citizen. It's an important document which gives you the following benefits:

- You will be able to apply for a Portuguese driving licence.
- You will be able to start a new business if you wish to.

In order to apply for a residence permit, you will require your visa. You will also be required to make what is known as an 'official request' on a questionnaire. You will need a certificate of your consular registration (or a written statement in case you do not have a certificate) together with other information which will depend on your current situation in Portugal:

- If you are in paid employment, you will need a legalised copy of your contract of employment.
- If you are hoping to establish a business, then you'll need a final decision relating to the business you wish to establish provided by the Foreign Investment Institute.
- If you are a pensioner or of independent means, a copy of your latest bank account statement.

Your application will then go to Lisbon and provided there are no hitches, your residence permit will turn up in due course.

Your initial permit (which is called Type A) will be valid for 12 months and there will be specified dates between which you can apply to renew it (and you should renew it on time as it could lapse if you are more than six months overdue). You should take it to the *Servicos de Estrangeiros* and it is renewed quite easily by filling in a simple form and providing evidence of your financial position. Once you have renewed your Type A *residencia* for five consecutive years, you can if you wish apply for a five year residence permit (called Type B). With a type A residence permit, you may purchase more than one house; with a five year type B residence permit, you have no restrictions on the acquisition of agricultural land either.

Making the move

Once you've bought your property in Portugal, then you're going to have to furnish it. You will of course find that Portugal, like every other European country, has all the furniture that you will ever need on offer at a wide variety of prices. Nevertheless, many people do like to bring their memories from home with them and in some cases, your second-hand furniture will be much cheaper than buying new furniture in Portugal.

If you are intending to buy property in Portugal then it's better to buy on the understanding that you are able to furnish it yourself rather than buying a fully furnished house in Portugal full of furniture that you don't particularly want. Then it's important to check on the rules and regulations for importing furniture before you sign the contract. The rules do tend to change from time to time so it would be worth your while checking at the Portuguese Consulate for up-to-date information.

Decree Law 467/88 of 16 December now regulates the importation of all personal goods including motor cars by EEC residents into Portugal. Similarly, Decree Law 31/89 of 25 January 1989 regulates the importation of such goods by non-EEC residents. A distinction is made between persons taking up permanent residence in Portugal and those merely wishing to furnish a second home.

Obtaining a baggage certificate

Before you can import your household and personal effects into Portugal, free of duty, you will need to obtain a baggage certificate.

Holiday homes

In order to obtain a baggage certificate to import furniture and other items for your holiday home, you will have to provide:

- A letter from your local authority stating that you are on the National Register of Electors of that area.
- An inventory of the goods you intend to import showing the value of each item and also proving that you've owned the items for at least three months.
- Proof of ownership of a home in Portugal (which will usually be the certificate of registration or the *caderneta predial*).

If you are taking up permanent residence in Portugal, in addition to the inventory and proof of ownership, you will also have to provide a certificate from the local authority stating that you are no longer on the Register of Electors and a copy of your resident's permit.

In order to satisfy the requirements of the authorities, it is very important to remember that these documents must be produced within 90 days of their date of issue.

The inventory (and you will need two copies) is quite simply a list of all the goods that you wish to take into Portugal. It must be in Portuguese (there will normally be some form of translation service in any major town but if not, then the shipper can normally arrange for this to be done for you). The list should simply be a list of all your possessions, the address where they're being taken from and the address in Portugal where they're being taken to. It should list all your main items of furniture together with any miscellaneous items such as china, glassware etc. Electrical items are rather more important – you must make sure that they are listed separately and describe them as accurately as possible (for example, give the maker's name and serial number).

There's a particular quirk regarding television sets. You

should firstly take note of the fact that they will normally have to be adapted for use in Portugal (Portugal is still on the old 405 line system) and secondly, you must also arrange for a completed Portuguese television licence application form to accompany the import documents.

Whether you are taking up permanent residence or merely wanting to import furniture for your second home, you will also have to file an Affidavit stating that you are aware that you must not sell or otherwise part with possession of the imported goods within the statutory period (2 years if you are taking up permanent residence or 1 year if it is furniture for a holiday home) and that you are aware that you will have to pay duty on those goods if you do not comply with this rule. It must give your address in Portugal and must declare that you have no other accommodation on Portuguese territory.

Finally, when both copies of the inventory and the affidavit have been signed in front of a notary they should be sent to the Portuguese Consul, requesting the baggage certificate. You can either do this in writing or go into the Consulate yourself. You must check the period of validity with the Consulate.

You may import your household and personal effects either in one go or several shipments. However, if you are taking up permanent residence, the last shipment must not be later than 12 months from the date that you have taken up normal residence in Portugal. If you later decide to retire in Portugal and take up permanent residence in your holiday home you may on this occasion import other household effects providing these have been in your possession for at least a period of 12 months. You must again ensure that the last shipment of these goods arrives in Portugal within 12 months from when you took up permanent residence.

On arriving in Portugal

When you finally arrive in Portugal, you will be asked to complete a declaration confirming that when you arrive you have no furnished residence there and that you are only bringing into the country the goods that have been mentioned on the inventory. Before you can get clearance of your furniture, you will have to take this declaration together with your **stamped** passport to the Portuguese customs and they will then release your furniture. They will also charge you something even though your goods are being imported free. The charge is based on the weight and value of the consignment (and to help on this it would be useful to attach a value to each item on the inventory) and it can cost as much as £500.

When you arrive in Portugal, you will also need to obtain a document, signed and notarised, in which you undertake not to dispose of the goods in any way whatsoever within one year from the official date of importation. If you are bringing particularly valuable items into the country, this period may be extended to 10 years.

The rules on duty-free goods

You will be able to import your furniture and other household goods free of customs duty if they are imported within 90 days either before or after your arrival in Portugal. It's most important that you have the required documentation because if you don't, there will be hold ups and this may stop the goods being cleared for importation into the country. In extreme circumstances, they may then be seized and auctioned by the customs authorities.

If you have inherited furniture and household goods after taking up residence in Portugal, you may import these under the provisions of article 10 of Decree Law 467/88 of 16 December 1988.

The final condition is that the importation must be completed in a maximum of *two* shipments. You will be able to get more information from the Portuguese Consulate in London and you should always talk to them first.

It's most important to keep all the evidence of correspondence and signed forms as a safety precaution in order to avoid subsequent misunderstandings.

Using a removal firm

In view of all the problems of importation, it could be very worth your while relying on a removal company of international experience as they will be familiar with the requirements of applying for a baggage certificate and also with the procedures at the customs points. It's advisable to get quotations from as many removal companies as you can and ask them also for the names of clients they have helped to move to Portugal.

Alternatively, if you decide not to use the removal firm, you may find that you might need the services of a customs agent in order to help you with the formalities. However, you should realise that the **customs agent** is not a customs **official** and so you will need from the agent a full set of receipts for any money you pay him showing what duties he has paid on your behalf and what are his charges for making the arrangements,

Insurance

Another point you should consider is the insurance of your goods in transit. If you are using a removal firm, you will probably find on reading the small print of the contract that the removal firm will absolve itself of all responsibility for damage or loss and rely on the insurers to pick up the bill for any damage.

You may be tempted to declare low values for your goods for the sake of paying a small customs charge when entering Portugal. However, you can't insure the goods for higher values than you have declared. It makes sense therefore to be realistic in your valuation and not to declare a low value which could lead to problems if the goods are damaged in transit.

Cars

The tourist

As a tourist, you can drive your own car freely in Portugal on your own UK driving licence (although it still makes sense to get an international driving licence to be on the safe side). It's not necessary to have a 'green card' but this might be the simplest way of complying with the Portuguese requirements that you must have at least 700,000 *escudos* minimum third party insurance. Also, if you are driving your car to Portugal, you must of course consider the requirements for licences and insurance required in the countries that you travel through on your way. If you are taking a car into Portugal which is not registered in your name you should have a letter of authority from the owner and you should contact the Portuguese Consul for information on getting the documentation authorised.

You may keep a foreign registered car in Portugal for up to six months although it is possible in certain cases to get a six month extension.

The resident

As a resident (ie when you've obtained a resident's visa), you must either re-export a foreign registered car or import it permanently. As an EEC resident you may, on taking up residence in Portugal, import a car for your own use. You may also import caravans, boats, mobile homes and private aeroplanes so long as they too are only for your private use. You will need to produce to the customs officials the registration documents eg log book etc.

Driving licence

For temporary visits, a valid UK driving licence or international driving licence is valid but foreigners living in Portugal with a residence permit must obtain a Portuguese driving licence. All residents of Portugal who apply for a driving licence now will be issued with the new pink European licence. If you are about to take up residence in Portugal and already hold such a licence then your probably don't need to change it. However, that's not entirely clear and it might be better to check with the Portuguese Consul before moving to Portugal.

Business and work

If you intend looking for temporary employment in Portugal, then it's a relatively straightforward process but for it to be officially authorised, the contract of temporary employment has to be registered with the Portuguese Minister of Labour. The application has to be made by a Portuguese company or a person resident in Portugal and they must be able to prove that they have made you a *bona fide* offer of employment. The contract must not run for more than six months but it can be renewed every six months for up to a total contracted period of three years.

For permanent work, you will first have to satisfy the authorities that you have made the necessary applications for a resident's visa and you will also need a work permit. This may take several months if it can be achieved at all. Application has to be made by your employer to the Minister of Labour but they will take great care to ensure that the ratio of Portuguese to foreign employees in any business follows the rules laid down by the Minister of Labour.

The rules for issuing work permits are complicated and they vary across the country. At the end of the day, the granting of a work permit is often at the discretion of local officials according to their view of the labour market in their own areas. In some areas, you will not get a work permit unless the work requires special skills or expertise which local Portuguese people do not possess. In all cases, it is advisable that you obtain competent legal advice when applying for a work permit.

If you are employed, it is a requirement that you have to pay Portuguese Social Security taxes on all remuneration received as a result of your employment in Portugal. Previously, expatriates continued to pay DSS contributions in the UK but this is no longer the case if you work in Portugal for more than three years. The Social Security tax is equal to 11% of your earnings and the benefits do not compare at all favourably with those provided in the UK.

If you intend to set up in self-employed business, then you don't require a work visa following the relaxation of controls when Portugal became a member of the EEC. However, if you intend to follow one of the professions you will need to provide evidence that you are actually entitled to follow that profession in the UK before you will be given a residence permit. If you intend to set up a more substantial business in Portugal, then you should get information from the Foreign Investment Institute.

Arranging your investments

Once you have settled down in Portugal, then you need to be reassured that you are going to have a ready source of income especially if you are dependent on income, such as a pension, from the UK. Under those circumstances, you will then have no difficulty at all in arranging payment of any personal or company pension to be paid direct to your bank account in Portugal (although some employers will probably prefer to pay it to a UK bank account and for you then to arrange a transfer to Portugal yourself).

If you go to live in Portugal before you have reached state retirement age (which is 65 for a man or 60 in the case of a woman) it would be sensible to arrange to continue to pay contributions in order to qualify for an old age pension. When you are working in the UK you will normally have paid class I contributions (class II is self-employed). When you are in Portugal, it will be sensible to continue to pay class III (non-employed contributions) in order to ensure that you qualify for your full pension.

Your local office of the DSS will be able to supply you with the necessary information. You should then make application to the DSS, overseas group in Newcastle Upon Tyne who will then make arrangements for you to continue paying your class III contributions (and the simplest method is by a single yearly instalment paid to a British bank).

Provided that you have been credited with the required number of contributions throughout your working life, then you will receive your old age pension at state retirement age. British pensioners in Portugal receive exactly the same pension they would have if they were living in Britain and they are entitled to the annual increase based on increases in the British cost of living.

16 Health and health insurance

Holiday insurance for tourists

For the holiday maker, health insurance is no problem. There are a number of British insurance companies that offer inexpensive holiday cover and your travel agent will always be pleased to give you details. It's a small expense which you shouldn't neglect to indulge yourself in. Good health, or an accident free life, can never be guaranteed – and holidays are no exception. It also pays you to insure your luggage because it is not entirely unknown for your holiday belongings to disappear between your home and your holiday home.

Reciprocal medical care

Reciprocal medical care is available to you in the EEC if you're a short-stay visitor eg if you're on holiday, or abroad on family visits. Treatments are usually limited to urgent cases of illness or accident and it is provided free or at a reduced cost depending on the health care schemes operating in each country.

Full details of treatments available can be found in DHSS Leaflet SA30 1986 which you should read carefully. You should complete form CMI (which is in the leaflet) and apply to your DSS office for certificate E111. If you are taken ill in Portugal, you can obtain reciprocal medical care by presenting your passport and certificate E111 (which is valid for up to two years).

Under the reciprocal arrangements, you will be entitled to treatment but only for conditions needing **immediate** attention during the visit. Arrangements for free or reduced cost treatment only apply if similar treatment would be provided by doctors or hospitals in the UK. Not all costs are refundable but the local sickness office in Portugal will pay those that are. If you have to have treatment, make sure the necessary documents are produced and tell the doctor/ hospital that you wish to be treated under the EC Social Security regulations. Also, apply for a refund before you return to the UK because you might find it very difficult to recover the expenses once you've left Portugal. You will get in-patient treatment in the general ward of an official hospital free of charge; you may have to pay for medical consultation at an official health centre, prescribed medicines and dental treatment.

Medical provision for residents

For the resident, the position is not quite so straightforward. Unless you are a pensioner, you won't have access to the Portuguese health service and so it is most important that you take out (or continue) private medical arrangements.

Pensioners

Under the European Community Social Security regulations, pensioners are entitled to health care from doctors and hospitals through the Portuguese social insurance scheme under the same terms as those which apply to Portuguese pensioners.

These new rules came into force on 1 January 1986 so if you are a resident in Portugal who has been subject to a pension deduction under the previous agreement between Britain and Portugal, then you should ensure that this deduction is no longer being made. If the DSS has not already written to you on form OVB–510 then you should contact the DSS overseas branch in Newcastle Upon Tyne.

In certain cases, British pensioners have considered it advantageous to exchange all their social security rights in the UK (both health **and** pension) for equivalent rights in Portugal. That decision may well depend on your age and also your record of National Insurance contributions while you were living in the UK but it could be worth your while getting information from both the DSS overseas branch and the authorities in Portugal.

Non-pensioners

As a non-pensioner, you won't be able to claim any benefits under the Portuguese national health system, and you will, as previously mentioned, have to make arrangements for private medical insurance before you are able to obtain your residence permit. You should of course maintain your DSS contributions in order to ensure that you qualify for a UK pension when you reach state retirement age.

If you are resident in Portugal and approaching the normal state retirement age for a UK pension, then you should write and get form E121 (also from the DSS overseas branch) which should then be sent to the relevant authorities.

Limits to the DSS benefits

It's tempting to believe that even though you live in Portugal, you can always use the UK as a last resort if you decide to have that major operation that you have been needing for years. However, that may not necessarily be the case. Although you remain eligible for sickness and invalidity benefits when you **return** to the UK (provided your National Insurance contributions are up to date), your entitlement to receive these benefits only lasts as long as you remain 'ordinarily resident', ie that you actually live in the UK.

Even if you continue to pay National Insurance contributions from abroad to ensure your entitlement to the full basic state retirement pension, those contributions don't automatically give you access to free health care if you return to the UK for a visit. If it is an **emergency**, then you are entitled to it free under the National Health Service, but DHSS leaflet SA34 points out that if the treatment is not an emergency, then you will have to pay for it. Yet another reason for maintaining your private medical insurance.

Medical insurance

There are, of course, a number of companies in the UK which will give you medical insurance whilst you are living in Portugal. It could be that you are already in a suitable scheme and it may be possible for you to extend it to cover your residence in Portugal. If you are not already in the scheme (and even if you are) it could pay you to shop around because all the schemes are different in relation to the benefits that they will provide once you make a move out of the UK.

The choice of which company to go for can only be made by you in the light of your own personal circumstances but the following checklist will give you an idea of the sorts of things that you might think about when choosing the insurance cover that suits you best:

- Will it restrict your travel abroad?
- Will it cover repatriation costs in the event of major illness or death?
- Are there any exclusions for particular sports?
- Are there any exclusions for illnesses you have had in the past?
- Are there any illnesses that are not covered (eg alcohol abuse)?

- Is there any type of treatment not covered (eg routine dental treatment)?
- Will it cover the cost of prescriptions?
- What level of hospital costs are covered?
- Will it cover nursing costs?
- Will it cover other members of your family?
- Is there an age limit to joining the scheme?
- Is there an age limit to the benefits provided by the scheme?
- Will the costs increase sharply when you reach a certain age?
- Is there a qualification period for membership in order to be able to start claiming benefits?

Old age

The provision of facilities for the **active** retired person has been a growing Portuguese industry in recent years. Unfortunately, little has been done for infirm and elderly foreigners because it has been almost impossible for health care professionals from other countries to work in Portugal. Consequently, many long-stay residents are packing their bags for the last time and returning home because of their increasing infirmity. For them, Portugal has lost its attraction because they will only feel comfortable about growing old 'back home'.

Many of the more elderly retired find it difficult to remain fully integrated with the Portuguese way of life and sometimes the problems of communication become greater with increasing age. Being able to share a common lifestyle is very important to older people and there is a strong case for the provision of care for elderly Britons by professionals from Britain who fully understand their needs. There are apartments with help on call, private rest homes and homes providing total care but they are few and far between and they can often be expensive for a retired person.

This is not meant to be gloomy – it's meant to inject a note of realism. Returning to Britain after a long stay abroad can be a difficult experience in itself and like any house move, it is better to make this kind of major decision whilst you are still fit enough to cope with the inevitable hassle that is going to materialise. Returning to Britain in your early 70s might be a wrench; returning to Britain in your early 80s could be a major problem.

Provision for death

When a person dies abroad, his relatives have several choices. The body can be embalmed and transported back to the UK for burial but this can be extremely expensive. As an alternative, arrangements can be made for burial in Portugal; the cemeteries are almost all Catholic but persons of any religion can be buried there. There are certain Protestant cemeteries but these are very few and far between.

The other alternative is cremation (which has recently been legalised in Portugal) but in practice this is difficult to arrange because of the lack of crematoria.

Index